SÖZLER PUBLICATIONS

Translated from the Turkish 'Hutbe-i Şâmiye'
by Şükran Vahide, Staff-writer of Nur-The Light

Second (revised and expanded) edition 1996.

For information, address:
Sözler Neşriyat A.Ş., Nuruosmaniye Cad., Sorkun Han 28/2,
Cağaloğlu, Istanbul, Turkey.
Tel: 0212 527 76 07; Fax: 0212 520 8231

Printed at: Sözler Ofset A.Ş.
Istanbul, 1996.

From the
Risale-i Nur Collection

THE
DAMASCUS
SERMON

by

Bediuzzaman
SAID NURSI

Contents

Contents

Who was Bediuzzaman Said Nursi and what is the Risale-i Nur?

Bediuzzaman Said Nursi was born in eastern Turkey in 1877 and died in 1960 at the age of eighty-three after a life of exemplary struggle and self-sacrifice in the cause of Islam. He was a scholar of the highest standing having studied not only all the traditional religious sciences but also modern science and had earned the name Bediuzzaman, Wonder of the Age, in his youth as a result of his outstanding ability and learning.

Bediuzzaman's life-time spanned the final decades of the Caliphate and Ottoman Empire, its collapse and dismemberment after the First World War, and, after its formation in 1923, the first thirty-seven years of the Republic, of which the years up to 1950 are famous for the government's repressive anti-Islamic and anti-religious policies.

Until the years following the First World War, Bediuzzaman's struggles in the cause of Islam had been active and in the public domain. He had not only taught many students and had engaged in debate and discussion with leading scholars from all over the Islamic world, but he had also commanded and led in person a volunteer regiment against the invading Russians in eastern Turkey in 1914 for nearly two years until taken prisoner. Furthermore, up to that time he had sought to further the interests of Islam by actively engaging in public life. However, the years that saw the transition from empire to republic also saw the transition from the 'Old Said' to the 'New Said'. The 'New Said' was characterized by his withdrawal from public life and concentration on study, prayer and thought, for what was required now was a struggle of a different sort.

Although he had paid no part in it, and in fact had strongly advised its leaders to abandon their uprising against the government, during the events in eastern Turkey of 1925, Bediuzzaman was sent into exile in western Anatolia. Following this, for the next twenty-five years, and to a lesser extent for the last ten years of his life, he suffered nothing but exile, imprisonment, harassment and persecution by the authorities. But these years of exile and isolation saw the writing of the Risale-i Nur, the Treatise of Light, and its dissemination throughout Turkey. To quote Bediuzzaman himself, "Now I see clearly that most of my life has been directed in such a way, outside my own free-will, ability, comprehension and foresight, that it might produce these treatises to serve the cause of the Qur'an. It is as if all my life as a scholar has been spent in preliminaries to these writings, which demonstrate the miraculousness of the Qur'an."

Bediuzzaman understood an essential cause of the decline of the Islamic world to be the weakening of its very foundations, that is, a weakening of belief in the basic tenets of the Islamic faith. This, together with the unprecedented attacks on those foundations in the 19th and 20th centuries carried out by materialists, atheists and others in the name of science and progress, led him to realize that the urgent and overriding need was to strengthen, and even to save, belief. What was needed was to expend all efforts to reconstruct the edifice of Islam from its foundations, belief, and to answer at that level those attacks with a 'non-physical jihad' or 'jihad of the word.'

Thus, in his exile, Bediuzzaman wrote a body of work, the Risale-i Nur, that would explain and expound the basic tenets of belief, the truths of the Qur'an, to modern man. His method was to analyse both belief and unbelief and to demonstrate through clearly reasoned arguments that not only is it possible, by following the method of the Qur'an, to prove rationally all the truths of belief, such as God's existence and unity, prophethood, and bodily resurrection, but also that these truths are the only rational explanation of existence, man and the universe.

Bediuzzaman thus demonstrated in the form of easily understood stories, comparisons, explanations, and reasoned proofs that, rather than the truths of religion being incompatible with the findings of modern science, the materialist interpretation of those findings is irrational and absurd. Indeed, Bediuzzaman proved in the Risale-i Nur that science's breathtaking discoveries of the universe's functioning corroborate and reinforce the truths of religion.

The importance of the Risale-i Nur cannot be over-estimated, for through it Bediuzzaman Said Nursi played a major role in preserving and revitalizing the Islamic faith in Turkey in the very darkest days of her history. And indeed its role has continued to increase in importance to the present day. But further to this, the Risale-i Nur is uniquely fitted to address not only all Muslims but indeed all mankind for several reasons. Firstly it is written in accordance with modern man's mentality, a mentality that, whether Muslim or not, has been deeply imbued by materialist philosophy: it specifically answers all the questions, doubts and confusions that this causes. It answers too all the 'why's' that mark the questioning mind of modern man.

Also, it explains the most profound matters of belief, which formerly only advanced scholars studied in detail, in such a way that everyone, even those to whom the subject is new, may understand and gain something without it causing any difficulties or harm.

A further reason is that in explaining the true nature and purpose of man and the universe, the Risale-i Nur shows that true happiness is only to be found in belief and knowledge of God, both in this world and the hereafter. And it also points out the grievous pain and unhappiness that unbelief causes man's spirit and conscience, which generally the misguided attempt to block out through heedlessness and escapism, so that anyone with any sense may take refuge in belief.

TO CONCLUDE:

The Holy Qur'an addresses the intellect as well as man's other inner faculties. It directs man to consider the universe and its functioning in order to learn its true nature and purposes as the creation and thus to learn the attributes of its Single Creator and his own duties as a creature. This, then, is the method that Bediuzzaman employed in the Risale-i Nur. He explained the true nature of the universe as signs of its Creator and demonstrated through clear arguments that when it is read as such all the fundamentals of belief may be proved rationally.

When this method is followed, a person attains a true belief that will be sound and firm enough to withstand any doubts that may arise in the face of the subtle attacks of Materialism, Naturalism and atheism, or the materialist approach to scientific advances. For all scientific and technological advances are merely the uncovering of the workings of the cosmos. When the cosmos is seen to be a vast and infinitely complex and meaningful unified book describing its Single Author, rather than causing doubt and bewilderment, all these discoveries and advances reinforce belief, they deepen and expand it.

Man's most fundamental need is the need for religion, the need to recognize and worship Almighty God with all His Most Beautiful Names and attributes, and to obey His laws; those manifest in the universe and those revealed through His prophets. In explaining the message of the Qur'an, Almighty God's final Revealed Book, brought and perfectly expounded by His final Prophet, Muhammad (Upon whom be blessings and peace), and Islam, the complete and perfected religion for mankind, Bediuzzaman Said Nursi demonstrated in the Risale-i Nur that there is no contradiction or dichotomy between science and religion; rather, true progress and happiness for mankind can, and will, only be achieved in this way, the way of the Qur'an.

Sözler Publications

*　　*　　*

Publisher's Preface
to the Damascus Sermon

While visiting Damascus in early 1911, Bediuzzaman Said Nursi was invited by the religious authorities there to give a sermon in the historic Umayyad Mosque. On their insistence he agreed, and delivered a sermon to a gathering of close on ten thousand, including one hundred scholars. It met with such a response that the text was afterwards printed twice in one week.

In this sermon, Bediuzzaman gave certain news that in the future Islam and the truths of the Qur'an would prevail, and he provided clear proofs that this would occur. Not only did he demonstrate how the Islamic world could heal itself through taking the medicines of the Qur'an, but he also pointed out a number of developments in the West, among them the stirrings of a genuine search for the truth, that indicated to a forthcoming acceptance of Islam. With extraordinary foresight, Bediuzzaman predicted that, as all the evidence suggested, Islam would in the near future gain ascendancy. However, the two World Wars and a period of despotism both in Turkey and elsewhere in the Islamic world, which he had not foreseen, delayed matters. That is to say, as the developments of which he gave news in 1911 slowly unfold, this sermon, together with its diagnosis of some of the fundamental ills afflicting the Islamic world and the remedies from the Holy Qur'an that it points out, continues to be of the greatest relevance for Muslims of the present day.

As Bediuzzaman Said Nursi demonstrates, since Islam relies on reason and reasoned proof, it is the religion of the present and the future, for this is the age of science, technology and reason. This fact is being understood now by many who realize that they cannot live without a true and complete religion. The causes for the decline of the Islamic world and its material backwardness in comparison to the West should be sought in the failure of Muslims to adhere to the teachings and truths of the Holy Qur'an and Islam. Just as Islam provides for the material progress of man, and the indeed urges him towards it, so does it provide for man's true progress and development in moral and spiritual matters. This combination forms the basis of true civilization.

Since Western civilization is not based on truth and justice, but on the principles of force, conflict, and aggression, the evils of civilization predominate over its virtues. If man is to survive he will embrace Islam, for he understands now his need for true civilization, founded on the positive truths of revelation, the Holy Qur'an and the Shari'a of the Prophet Muhammad (PBUH), in which the virtues of progress predominate, and the benefits of civilization may be profited from.

In the form of "Six Words," Bediuzzaman describes a number of those positive truths of Islam, which form the cure for the grievous sicknesses besetting the Muslim community. Hope, courage, honesty, love and brotherhood, self-sacrifice, awareness of the luminous bonds uniting the believers, mutual consultation. These are not qualities that are unimportant or may be dispensed with in the face of the difficulties or threats; on the contrary, they form the very foundation of Muslim society.

As the truths of the Qur'an and Islam become increasingly apparent in this age of scientific discovery and technological advance, the lessons of Bediuzzaman Said Nursi's prophetic sermon of 1911 increase in significance. The civilization of the future is true civilization; the civilization of Islam. It will be achieved through Muslims heeding these lessons, and rebuilding their society on the foundations of belief, and on the morality of Islam.

Besides the two original printings of the Sermon, a further edition of the Arabic text was published in Istanbul in 1922. In the 1950's it was translated into Turkish by the author, and then published as part of the Risale-i Nur Collection. Bediuzzaman expanded to some degree this Turkish edition, which is the source of the present translation, in order to address directly contemporary Muslims also. For this reason there are references to dates subsequent to 1911, and to other parts of the Risale-i Nur.

Bediuzzaman added other pieces to the Turkish edition, taken from various of his works, which all illustrate aspects of the main theme of his sermon, that not only Muslims, but all mankind, will find happiness and salvation only through applying the principles of the Qur'an in their social and political lives. It will also be useful for readers to bear in mind that Bediuzzaman saw the achievement of this through the spread of the healing light of the Qur'anic teachings on the truths of belief — exemplified in the Risale-i Nur— and their acceptance, rather than as a result of political activity.

* * *

Introduction

to the Turkish Translation of the Original Arabic 'Damascus Sermon'

In His Name, be He glorified!
And there is nothing but it glorifies Him with praise

Peace be upon you and God's mercy and blessings for ever!

My Dear, Loyal Brothers!

[With a presentiment of the future, the Old Said perceived the truths expressed in this Arabic sermon, which, on the insistence of the Damascus religious authorities, he delivered forty years ago in the Umayyad Mosque to a congregation of close on ten thousand, which included a hundred religious scholars; he gave news of those truths with complete certainty as though they were going to be realized shortly. However, the two World Wars and twenty-five years of absolute despotism delayed their realization; it is now that the signs of this, which were predicted then, are beginning to be seen in the world of Islam. Therefore, if you consider it appropriate, you may publish the translation of this most important and instructive piece, not as an old, outdated

17

sermon, but as fresh and correct instruction on social
and Islamic questions addressing directly, in 1371
instead of 1327, the congregation of three hundred and
seventy (now more than a million) million in the
mosque of the Islamic world, rather than in the
Umayyad Mosque.]

I t is fitting here to write the most important answer
to a most important question. For the Old Said
spoke prophetically in that lesson of forty years
ago as though he was seeing the wondrous teachings of
the Risale-i Nur and its effects. It is for this reason that I
am writing that question and answer here. It is like this:

Many have asked both me and the Risale-i Nur students: "Why is it that the Risale-i Nur is not defeated in
the face of so much opposition and so many obdurate philosophers and people of misguidance? By preventing to
an extent the dissemination of numerous valuable and
true books on belief and Islam, and by means of their
worldly pleasures and vices, they have deprived many
youths and others of the truths of belief. But their most
violent attacks, vicious treatment, lies and propaganda
have been directed at the Risale-i Nur, to destroy it and to
scare people away from it and to give it up. Despite this,
the Risale-i Nur has spread in a way never seen in any
other work, six hundred thousand copies of its treatises
being written out by hand with unflagging zeal and published secretly. How is it that it causes itself to be read
with such enthusiasm, both within the country and
abroad? What is the reason for it? In reply to the many
questions of this sort, we say:

Being a true commentrary on the All-Wise Qur'an
through the mystery of its miraculousness, the Risale-i
Nur demonstrates that in misguidance is a sort of Hell in

this world, while in belief is a sort of Paradise. It points out the grievous pains in sins, bad deeds, and forbidden pleasures, and proves that in good deeds and virtues and the truths of the Shari'a are to be found pleasures like the pleasures of Paradise. In this way it saves the sensible among those who have fallen into vice and misguidance. For at this time there two awesome conditions:

T h e   F i r s t : Since man's emotions, which are blind to the consequences of things and prefer an ounce of present pleasure to tons of future joys, have prevailed over his mind and reason, the only way to save the dissipated from their vice is to show them the pain present in their pleasure and to defeat their emotions. Although they are aware of the diamond-like bounties and pleasures of the hereafter, as the verse, *They deem lovable the life of this world*[1] indicates, while being believers, the people of misguidance choose worldly pleasures, which are like pieces of glass soon to be shattered. The only way of saving them from this love of the world and from the danger of succumbing to it is by showing them the hell-like torments and pains they suffer even in this world. This is the way the Risale-i Nur takes. For at this time, due to the obduracy arising from absolute unbelief and the intoxication caused by the vice and misguidance arising from science, perhaps only one in ten or even twenty can be induced to give up his evil ways by proving the existence of Hell and its torments, after having told him of Almighty God. Having heard this, such people are likely to say: "God is Forgiving and Compassionate, and Hell is a long way off," and continue in their dissipation. Their hearts and spirits are overcome by their emotions.

Thus, by showing through most of its comparisons the

---

1. Qur'an, 14:3.

grievous and terrible results in this world of disbelief and
misguidance, the Risale-i Nur makes even the most stub-
born and arrogant people feel disgust at those inauspicious, illicit pleasures, leading them to repent. The
short comparisons in the Sixth, Seventh, and Eighth
Words, and the long one in the Third Stopping-Place in
the Thirty-Second Word induce a person feel repugnance
at the vice and misguidance of the way he has taken, and
cause him to accept what they teach. As an example, I
shall recount briefly the situations I beheld on a journey
of the imagination, which were in fact reality. Those
wishing for a more detailed account may look at the end
of *Sikke-i Tasdik-i Gaybi* (The Ratifying Stamp of the
Unseen Collection).

When on that journey of the imagination I looked at the
animal kingdom through the eyes of materialist philosophy and of the people of misguidance and heedlessness, the innumerable needs of animals and their terr-
rible hunger together with their weakness and impotence
appeared to me as most piteous and grievous. I cried out.
Then I saw through the telescope of Qur'anic wisdom and
belief that the Divine Name of All-Merciful had risen in
the sign of Provider like a shining sun; it gilded with the
light of its mercy that hungry, wretched animal world.

Then I saw within the animal world another grievous
world which was swathed in darkness and would make
anyone feel pity in which young were struggling in their
need and powerlessness. I was sorry I had looked through
the eyes of the people of misguidance. Suddenly, belief
gave me other spectacles and I saw the Name of All-
Compassionate rise in the sign of clemency; it transformed and lit up that pitiful world in joyous and beautiful fashion, changing my tears of complaint and sorrow
into tears of joy and thanks.

Then the world of humanity appeared to me as though on a cinema screen. I looked through the telescope of the people of misguidance and saw that world to be so dark and terrifying that I cried out from the depths of my heart. "Alas!" I cried. For they had desires and hopes that stretched to eternity, thoughts and imaginings that embraced the universe, the earnest desire for everlasting happiness and Paradise, an innate capacity and powers on which no limit had been placed and which were free, yet despite their innumerable needs and their weakness and impotence they were exposed to the attacks of innumerable enemies and the blows of innumerable calamities. Under the perpetual threat of death, they lived out their brief and tumultuous lives in wretched circumstances. Ever looking to the grave, which for the misguided is the door to everlasting darkness, they suffered the continuous blows of death and separation, the most painful state for the heart and conscience. I saw that singly and in groups they were being thrown into that black well.

On seeing the world of humanity in this darkness I was about to cry out with my heart, spirit, and mind, and all my subtle inner faculties, indeed all the particles of my being, when the light and power of belief proceeding from the Qur'an smashed those spectacles of misguidance, giving me insight. I saw the Divine Name of All-Just rising like the sun in the sign of All-Wise, the Name of All-Merciful rising in the sign of Munificent, the Name of All-Compassionate rising in the sign of, that is, in the meaning of, All-Forgiving, the Name of Resurrector rising in the sign of Inheritor, the Name of Giver of Life rising in the sign of Bountiful, and the Name of Sustainer rising in the sign of Owner. They lit up the entire world of humanity and all the worlds within it. They dispelled those hell-like states, opened up windows onto the luminous worlds of the hereafter, and scattered lights over the world of humanity. I declared: "Praise and thanks be to God to the number of particles in existence!" I understood with complete certainty that in belief is a sort of paradise in this world too and in misguidance, a sort of hell.

Then the world of the earth appeared. On that journey of the imagination, the dark, hypothetical rules of the philosophy which does not obey religion depicted a ghastly world. Voyaging through space on the ship of the aged earth —which travels seventy times faster than a cannonball a distance of twenty-five thousand years in one year, ever disposed to break up, its interior in a state of upheaval— the situation of wretched human kind appeared to me in a desolate darkness. My eyes darkened. I flung the spectacles of philosophy to the ground, smashing them. Then I looked with an eye illuminated with the wisdom of the Qur'an and belief, and I saw the Names of Creator of the Heavens and Earth, All-Powerful, All-Knowing, Sustainer, Allah, Sustainer of the Heavens and Earth, Subjugator of the Sun and Moon had risen like suns in the signs of mercy, tremendousness, and dominicality. They lit up that dark, desolate, and terrifying world so that the globe appeared to my eye of belief as a most well-ordered, subjugated, pleasant, and safe ship, or aeroplane or train. It contained everyone's provisions, and had been decked out for trade and enjoyment and to carry beings with spirits through the dominical realms around the sun. I exclaimed: "All praise be to God to the number of particles of the earth for the bounty of belief."

This has been proved with many comparisons in the Risale-i Nur, that those who follow vice and misguidance suffer a hellish torment in this world too, while through the manifestations of belief, the believers and righteous may taste through the stomachs of Islam and humanity the pleasures of Paradise. They may benefit according to the degree of their belief. But in these stormy times, currents which numb the senses and scatter man's attention on peripheral matters, plunging him into them, have deadened his senses and bewildered him. As a result of this the people of misguidance are temporarily unable to feel their torment, while the people of guidance are overwhelmed by heedlessness and cannot truly appreciate its pleasures.

The Second Awesome Condition This Age: In former times, compared with the present there was very little absolute disbelief, or misguidance arising from science, or the disbelief arising from perverse obstinacy. The instruction of the Islamic scholars of those times and their arguments were therefore sufficient, quickly dispelling any unbelief arising from doubts. Belief in God was general, and they could persuade most people give up their misguidance and wrongdoing through teaching them about God and reminding them of Hell-fire. But now there are a hundred absolute disbelievers in one small town instead of perhaps one in a whole country. Those who lose their way due to science and learning and obstinately oppose the truths of belief have increased a hundredfold in relation to former times. With pride like that of the Pharaoh and their terrible misguidance these obdurate deniers oppose the truths of belief. A sacred truth is therefore much needed that will completely destroy the bases of their disbelief in this world, like an atom bomb, and will halt their aggression and bring some of them to belief.

All praise be to Almighty God that with its many comparisons, as the perfect remedy for the wounds of this time, the Risale-i Nur —a miracle of the Qur'an of Miraculous Exposition proceeding from its effulgence— has routed even the most worst of those obdurate deniers with the diamond sword of the Qur'an. Its proofs and arguments to the number of the atoms of the universe demonstrating Divine Unity and the truths of belief show that in twenty-five years it has not been defeated in the face of the severest attacks, but has itself prevailed and been victorious. Yes, with its comparisons of belief and unbelief, and guidance and misguidance, the Risale-i Nur proves those truths self-evidently. If note is taken for example of the proofs and flashes of the Second Station of the Twenty-Second Word, the First Stopping-Place of the Thirty-Second Word, the 'Windows' of the Thirty-Third Letter, and the eleven proofs of *Asa-yı Musa* (The Staff of Moses), it will be understood that it is the truths of the Qur'an manifested in the Risale-i Nur that will smash and destroy absolute disbelief and perverse misguidance at this time.

In the same way that the parts of the Risale-i Nur solving the greatest mysteries of religion and the riddles of the world's creation have been collected together in *Tılsımlar Mecmuası* (The 'Mysteries' Collection), the pieces which describe the hell in this world of the people of misguidance and the paradise-like pleasures of the people of guidance and show that belief is like a seed of Paradise while unbelief is a seed of the Zakkum-tree of Hell, will be put together in a small collection, God willing, and published.

Said Nursi

* * *

The Damascus Sermon

We too offer the praise and thanks and gifts that all animate creatures offer through the tongues of their beings and lives to their Creator, the Necessarily Existent One, Who said:

Do not despair of God's mercy.[1]

And never-ending blessings and peace be upon our Prophet, Muhammad the Elect of God (Upon whom blessings and peace), who said:

"I came to perfect morality."[2]

That is, "An important reason for my being sent to mankind by Almighty God was to perfect good conduct and morality, and deliver mankind from immorality and vice."

---

1. Qur'an, 39:53.
2. 'Ajlūnī, *Kashf al-Khafā'*, i, 211.

Having offered praise to God and sought His blessings for His Messenger, I say this: O my Arab brothers who are listening here in the Umayyad Mosque! I have not mounted this pulpit, which is far above my station, in order to guide you, for to teach you is beyond my authority. I am like a child before this gathering, among whom are close on a hundred religious scholars, who goes to school in the morning and learns his lesson, then in the evening returns and repeats it to his father. His father sees whether or not what the child has learnt is correct, and the child awaits either approval or guidance from him. Yes, we are like children before you, and we are your students. You are our masters, and the masters of the other Muslim nations. I shall therefore repeat to you, our masters, part of the lesson I have learnt. It is as follows:

In the conditions of the present time in these lands, I have learnt a lesson in the school of mankind's social life and I have realized that what has allowed foreigners, Europeans, to fly towards the future on progress while it arrested us and kept us, in respect of material development, in the Middle Ages, are six dire sicknesses. The sicknesses are these:

FIRSTLY: The rising to life of despair and hopelessness in social life.

SECONDLY: The death of truthfulness in social and political life.

THIRDLY: Love of enmity.

FOURTHLY: Not knowing the luminous bonds that bind the believers to one another.

FIFTHLY: Despotism, which spreads, becoming widespread as though it was various contagious diseases.

SIXTHLY: Restricting endeavour to what is personally beneficial.

I shall explain, by means of six 'Words,' the lesson I have learnt from the pharmacy of the Qur'an, which is like a faculty of medicine. This lesson constitutes the medicine to cure our social life of those six dire sicknesses.

First Word

T he first word is 'hope;' that is, to nurture a strong hope of God's mercy. As a consequence of the lesson I have learnt on my own account, I say: O congregation of Muslims! I give you this good news: the first signs of the true dawn of Arab happiness are just appearing. This happiness will occur through the kindling of the worldly happiness of all Muslims, in particular that of the Ottomans, and especially through the progress of Islam. The emergence of the sun of happiness has drawn close. In order to rub despair's nose in the dust,[3] I say what is my firm conviction so that the world will hear:

The future shall be Islam's and Islam's alone. And its ruler shall be the truths of the Qur'an and belief. Therefore, we must submit to Divine Determining and our fate of the present, for ours is a brilliant future, while the

---

3. The Old Said, through a presentiment of the event, gave news forty-five years ago of what occurred in 1371/1951, namely that the Islamic world, and foremost the Arabic states, would be delivered from subjection to foreign powers and their despotism, and would form Islamic states. He did not think of the two World Wars and thirty to forty years of absolute despotism. He gave the good news of what actually occurred in 1371/1951 as though it would occur in 1327/1909. He did not take into account the reasons for the delay.

Europeans' is a dubious past. I shall now mention one and a half preliminary arguments. I start with the premises of those arguments:

Islam and its truths possess the perfect capacity to progress, both materially and in moral and non-material matters.

Progress in Moral and Non-Material Matters, which is the First Aspect

You should know that history, which records actual events, is the most faithful witness to the truth. See! History is showing us. The testimony of the Japanese Commander-in Chief who defeated Russia to the validity and justice of Islam is this:

"History shows that the Muslims increased in civilization and progressed in relation to the power of the truths of Islam; that is, to the degree that they acted in accordance with that power. History also shows that they fell into savagery and decline, and disaster and defeat amidst utter confusion to the degree of their weakness in adhering to the truths of Islam." As for other religions, it is quite to the contrary. That is to say, history shows that they increased in civilization and progressed in relation to their weakness in adhering to their religions and bigotry, and were subject to decline and revolution to the degree of their strength in adhering to them. Up to the present, time has passed thus.

Furthermore, from the blessed time of the Prophet (PBUH) up to the present, not a single event in history has shown us a Muslim who has embraced another religion, whether old or new, in preference to Islam, as result of reasoned argument and conclusive evidence. If the uneducated embrace another religion without evidence in blind imitation, it has no bearing on this matter. And to be without religion is yet another question. However, history shows us that followers of other religions, and even the English and pre-Revolution Russians, who displayed the greatest bigotry in religion, are gradually approaching and entering Islam on the strength of reasoned argument and cogent proofs, sometimes in groups.[4]

If we were to display through our actions the perfections of the morality of Islam and the truths of belief, without doubt the followers of other religions would enter Islam in whole communities; some entire regions and states, even, would take refuge in Islam.

Moreover, man has been awakened and aroused by the modern sciences in particular; he has understood the true nature of humanity.

Without any shadow of a doubt, man cannot live without religion, aimlessly. He cannot. Even the most irreligious person is compelled to take refuge in religion. For the only point of support for impotent man in the face of the innumerable disasters and the external and internal enemies that plague him, and the only point from which he may seek help and assistance in the face of the

---

4. Proofs of this claim, and powerful witnesses to it, are the following facts; that, forty-five years after this claim was made, in spite of two appalling world wars and the emergence of an extreme and absolute despotism, small northern states like Sweden, Norway and Finland have accepted and started to teach the Qur'an in their schools as a barrier to communism and irreligion. A number of prominent English orators are also seen to be in favour of encouraging the English to accept the Qur'an. And America, now the most powerful state on earth, is seen to support the truths of religion with all its strength, and has decided that Asia and Africa shall find prosperity, peace and reconcilation through Islam, and it patronizes and encourages the newly emergent Muslim states and tries to enter into alliance with them.

innumerable needs with which he is afflicted, and his desires that stretch to eternity, despite his utter want and poverty, is in recognizing the Maker of the world, in faith, and in believing and affirming the hereafter. There is no help for awakened mankind apart from this.

If the jewel of true religion is not present in the shell of the heart, material, moral, and spiritual calamities of untold magnitude will break loose over humanity and man will become the most unhappy, the most wretched, of animals.

In Short: This century, man has been awakened by the warnings of war, science, and awesome events, and he has perceived the true nature of humanity and his own comprehensive disposition. Man has begun to understand that with his wonderful comprehensive abilities and disposition, he was not created only for this brief and troublesome worldly life, but that he is a candidate for eternity, for there are within him desires that extend that far. Everybody has begun to realize that this narrow and transient world is not sufficient and cannot meet their boundless hopes and desires.

If it is said to the imagination, which is one of the faculties and servants of humanity: "You will rule the world and live for a million years, but in the end you will be despatched to non-existence with no possibility of a return to life," for sure, the imagination of one who has not lost his true humanity and who has been awakened, rather than being joyful and pleased, will weep longingly and with sighs and regrets at there being no eternal happiness.

Thus, included in this point is the fact that in everyone's heart an inclination has sprung up to search earnestly for a true religion. In the face of the sentence of death, before anything else man is searching for a truth, contained only in true religion, so that he may save himself. The present state of the world testifies to this fact.

After forty-five years and the appearance of irreligion, regions and states on the earth have begun to perceive, like a human being, this intense need of mankind. Furthermore, at their beginning and end, the verses of the Qur'an refer man to his reason, saying: "Use your intelligence! Think! Consult your mind and your heart! Confer with them so that you might know this fact!"

Look at the beginnings and ends of verses such as those; they say: "Why do you not look? Why do you not take warnings? Look so that you may know the truth." Take note of the way "Know!" is used. Many verses contain sentences that have the meaning of: "Why do men not know, why do they fall into compounded ignorance? Why do they not look? Have they become blind so that they cannot see the Truth? Why do men not call to mind and ponder over their own lives and the events in the world so that they might find the straight path? Why do they not think, deliberate and reason with the mind, and so fall into misguidance? O men! Take a lesson! Take a warning from past ages and try to be saved from the moral and spiritual calamities of the future!" These verses refer man to his intellect; they enjoin him to consult with his reason.

O my brothers in this Umayyad Mosque as well as those in the vast mosque of the world of Islam! You too take warning. Take warning from the dreadful events of the last forty-five years. Come straight to your senses! O you who are wise and thoughtful and consider yourselves to be enlightened!

Conclusion: We Muslims, who are students of the Qur'an, follow proof; we approach the truths of belief through reason, thought, and our hearts. We do not abandon proof in favour of blind obedience and imitation of the clergy like some adherents of other religions. *Therefore, in the future when reason, science and technology prevail, of a certainty that will be the time the Qur'an will gain ascendancy, which relies on rational proofs and invites the reason to confirm its pronouncements.*

Moreover, the veils that have eclipsed the sun of Islam, hindered its emergence and prevented it illuminating mankind have begun to disperse. Those things that were hindering it have begun to fall back. The signs of the dawn appeared forty-five years ago.[5] Then the true dawn broke in 1371/1951, or it will break. Even if it is the false dawn, in thirty or forty years' time the true dawn will break.

Eight serious obstacles prevented the truths of Islam completely overwhelming the past.

THE FIRST, SECOND, AND THIRD OBSTACLES: The Europeans' ignorance, their barbarity at that time, and their bigotry in their religion. These three obstacles have been removed by the virtues of knowledge and civilization, and they have begun to disperse.

THE FOURTH AND FIFTH OBSTACLES : The domination and arbitrary power of the clergy and religious leaders, and the fact that the Europeans obeyed and followed them blindly. These two obstacles have also started to disappear with the emergence among mankind of the idea of freedom, and the desire to search for the truth.

---

5. That is, in 1906. [Tr.]

THE SIXTH AND SEVENTH OBSTACLES : The despotism that was with us, and our degeneracy that arose from opposing the Shari'a, were obstacles. The fact that the separate despotic power residing in a single individal is now declining indicates that the fearful despotism of larger groups in society and of committees will also decline in thirty to forty years' time. And the great upsurge in Islamic zeal, together with the fact that the ugly results of immorality are becoming apparent, show that these two obstacles are about to decline, indeed, that they have begun to do so. God willing, they will completely disappear in the future.

THE EIGHTH OBSTACLE : Since certain matters of modern science were imagined to oppose and be contrary to the outer meanings of the truths of Islam, it prevented, to some extent, their prevailing in the past. Scientists and philosophers opposed Islam because they did not know the truth and, for example, imagined the two angels composed of spirit called Thawr and Hut, who are charged through a Divine command to oversee the globe of the earth, to be a great corporeal ox and fish.

There are hundreds of examples like this one. After learning the truth, even the most opinionated philosopher is compelled to submit to it. In the treatise called the Miraculousness of the Qur'an,[6] the Risale-i Nur points out flashes of the Qur'an's miraculousness that lie beneath each of all the verses that science attacks, and it sets forth clearly the elevated truths, which the hand of science cannot reach, in those sentences and phrases of the Holy Qur'an that the scientists suppose to be points of

---

6. The Twenty-Fifth Word. [Tr.]

criticism; it compels even the most obstinate philosopher to submit. It is clear and self-evident, anyone who wishes may look. —So let them look and see how this obstacle is being destroyed, as these words forecasted forty-five years ago.

Some perspicacious Muslim scholars have indeed written on this subject. Signs that this eighth serious obstacle will be overturned are to be seen.

For sure, even if not now then in thirty to forty years' time, in order to fit out and equip to perfection the three forces of science, true knowledge, and the virtues of civlization, and to rout and put to flight those eight obstacles, the desire to search for the truth, equity, and love of humanity will be despatched to the eight fronts of those eight enemy squadrons. They have already started to drive them back. God willing, in half a century they will scatter them completely.

It it well-known that the most indisputable virtue is that which even its enemies testify to and affirm. The following therefore are two examples out of hundreds:

The First: A famous European scholar and philosopher of the 19th century, Carlyle, did not hold back from proclaiming in the loudest voice to philosophers and Christian scholars the following, which he also wrote in his works, that Islam was born like a brilliant flame and devoured the religions of its time as though they were dead wood. It was Islam's right to do this he said, for it was a reality, while the other religions lacked reality. He said also that the words most worthy to be heeded first are those of Muhammad (Upon whom be blessings and peace), for the true word was his. He said too that if the truth of Islam is doubted then the most self-evident matters should be doubted, because the most self-evident and necessary truth is Islam.[7]

Second Example: A famous European of the last century who was also a scholar and philosopher, Prince Bismarck, said:

"I have studied all the revealed books, but since they are corrupted, I have been unable to find the true wisdom I was searching for, for the happiness of mankind. Then I saw that the Qur'an of Muhammad was far superior to all the other Books. I found wisdom in all its words. There is no other work that will serve man's happiness like this. Such a work cannot be the word of man. Those who say it is Muhammad's work are denying the imperatives of knowledge. That is, the Qur'an is self-evidently the word of God."

So, supported by the fact that the clever fields of Europe and America have produced crops of brilliant and exacting scholars like Carlyle and Bismarck, I say with all assurance:

Europe and America are pregnant with Islam; one day they will give birth to an Islamic state. Just as the Ottomans were pregnant with Europe and gave birth to a European state.

O my brothers who are here in the Umayyad Mosque and those who are in the mosque of the world of Islam half a century later! Do the introductory remarks, that is, those made up to here, not point to the conclusion that it is Islam that will be the true, and spiritual, ruler over the future, and only Islam that will lead mankind to happi-

---

7. Thomas Carlyle, 1795-1880. See his work, *On Heroes, Hero-Worship and the Heroic in History*, London, 1841, which is the transcript of six public lectures Carlyle gave in London in 1840, the second of which was entitled: The Hero as Prophet. Mahomet: Islam.

ness in this world and the next; and that true Christianity, stripping off superstition and corrupted belief, will be transformed into Islam; following the Qur'an, it will unite with Islam?

Second Aspect

That is, the powerful reasons for Islam's material progress show that Islam will also be materially dominant in the future. The First Aspect demonstrated its progress in moral and spiritual matters and this Second Aspect offers strong proofs for its material progress and supremacy in the future. For established in the heart of the Islamic world's collective personality are five extremely powerful, unbreakable 'Strengths,' which have blended and coalesced.[8]

First Strength: This is the reality of Islam, which is the master of all perfection, can make three hundred and seventy million souls as a single soul, has been furnished

---

8. We understand from the Qur'an's teaching and instruction and what these indicate, that through mentioning the prophets' miracles, the Qur'an is informing mankind that events similar to those miracles will come into existence in the future through progress, and is urging them to achieve them, saying:

"Come on work! Show examples of these miracles! Like the Prophet Solomon (UWP), cover a journey of two months in a day! Like the Prophet Jesus (UWP), work to discover the cure of the most frightful diseases! Like the Prophet Moses (UWP), extract the water of life from stone and deliver mankind from thirst! Like the Prophet Abraham (UWP), find materials and dress in them so that fire will not burn you! Like some of the prophets, listen to distant voices and see distant images in east and west! Like the Prophet David (UWP), soften iron like dough and make it like wax to meet the needs of mankind! How greatly you benefit from the clock and the ship, the miracles of the Prophet Joseph (UWP) and the Prophet Noah (UWP) respectively. Benefit in the same way from the miracles the other prophets taught you, and imitate them."

By analogy with the above, the Qur'an instructs mankind in every respect, urges them to material, moral and spritual progress, and proves that it is the universal teacher and master.

with a real civilization and positive, true sciences, and is such that it cannot be destroyed by any power.

Second Strength: An intense need, which is the real master of civilization and industry, and is the source and means of development, together with complete, back-breaking poverty, are such strengths that they may be neither silent nor crushed.

Third Strength: This Strength, which teaches men exalted aims in the form of competition for exalted things, and causes them to strive on that way, which shatters despotism, excites exalted emotions, and destroys jealousy, envy, malice and rivalry, and is furnished with true awakening, the eagerness of competition, the tendency towards renewal and predisposition for civilization, consists of the freedom which is accordance with the Shari'a. That is to say, it has been fitted out with the desire for the highest accomplishments worthy of humanity.

Fourth Strength: This the fearlessness arising from belief, which is decked out with compassion. That is, neither to demean oneself or to be servile to oppressors and despots, nor to oppress and be arrogant towards the unfortunate; these form the foundations of the freedom which is accordance with the Shari'a.

Fifth Strength: This is the dignity of Islam, which proclaims and upholds the Word of God. In this age, proclaiming the Word of God is contingent on material progress; it may be proclaimed only through ahieving true civilization. It cannot be doubted that in the future the world of Islam's collective personality will carry out to the letter that categorical command issued by the dignity of Islam through belief.

In the past, Islam's progress occurred through smashing

the enemy's bigotry and obstinacy and through defence
against their aggression; through weapons and the sword.
Whereas in the future, in place of weapons, the immaterial, moral swords of true civilization, material progress,
and truth and justice will defeat and scatter the enemies.

You should understand that what I mean are the good
things that are civilization's virtues and its benefits for
mankind. Not its iniquities and evils that idiots have imagined to be its virtues, and imitating them, devastated our
possessions. Giving religion as the bribe, they have not
even gained the world. Through civilization's iniquities
prevailing over its benefits and its evils being preferred to
its virtues, mankind has suffered two calamitous blows in
the form of two world wars, and overturning that sinful
civilization men have been so utterly disgusted that they
have smeared the face of the earth with blood.

God willing, through the strength of Islam in the
future, the virtues of civilization will prevail, the face of
the earth cleansed of filth, and universal peace be
secured.

Indeed, the facts that European civilization is not
founded on virtue and guidance, but on lust and passion,
rivalry and oppression, and that up to the present the evils
of civilization have predominated over its virtues, and
that it has been infiltrated by revolutionary societies like
a wormeaten tree, are each like powerful indications and
means for the supremacy of Asian civilization. In a short
period of time it will prevail.

How is it that while there are such powerful and
unshakeable ways and means for the material and moral
progress of the believers and people of Islam, and
although the road to future happiness has been opened up
like a railway, you despair and fall into hopelessness in

the face of the future, and destroy the morale of the Islamic world? In despair and hopelessness you suppose that "the world is the world of progress for Europeans and everyone else," but "it is the world of decline only for the unfortunate people of Islam!" By saying that you are making a grievous mistake.

Since the desire to progress and be perfected has been included in the universe and in man's essential nature, for sure, if doomsday does not soon engulf mankind as a result of its errors and wrongdoing, in the future truth and justice will show the way to a worldly happiness in the world of Islam, God willing, in which there will be atonement for the former errors of mankind.

Consider this: time does not run in a straight line so that its beginning and end draw apart from one another; it moves in a circle, like the motion of the globe of the earth. Sometimes it displays the seasons of spring and summer as progress, and sometimes the seasons of storms and winter as decline. Just as every winter is followed by spring and every night by morning, mankind also shall have a morning and a spring, God willing. You may expect from Divine mercy to see true civilization within universal peace brought about through the sun of the truth of Islam.

At the start of the lesson I said I would demonstrate one and a half arguments to support my assertion. Now, one argument, in concise form, is finished and the remaining half argument is as follows:

As has been established by the prying investigations and innumerable experiments of the sciences, the fundamental and absolutely overriding aim and the true purpose of the All-Glorious Maker in the order of the universe are good, beauty, excellence and perfection. For all

the physical sciences demonstrate such an order and perfection in the fields they study in accordance with their
comprehensive laws that the intellect can find nothing
more perfect.

For example, sciences such as anatomy in medicine,
the science of the solar system in astronomy, and botany
and biology, all demonstrate the miracles of power and
the wisdom of the All-Glorious Maker in the order in
their own particular fields, and the truth of the verse,

Who makes most excellent everything that He creates.[9]

Also, inductive reasoning and general experience demonstrate that evil, ugliness, defect, badness and futility
are minor in the creation of the universe. They are not the
aim; they are dependent and secondary. That is to say,
ugliness has not entered the universe for the sake of ugliness, but as a unit of measurement in order to transform a
single truth of beauty into numerous truths. Evil, and
Satan even, have been set to pester man in order to be the
means of his limitless progress through competition.
Minor evils and ugliness like these have been created in
the universe in order to be the means of instances of universal beauty and good. Thus, according to inductive reasoning, the true aim and result of creation prove that
good, beauty and being perfected are fundamental in the
universe and that they are the true aim. So since men
have filthied and disordered the face of the earth to this
degree with their wicked godlessness and depart this
world without receiving their deserts and without reflect-
ing the true aim present in the universe, they certainly
shall not escape to non-existence. They shall rather be
despatched to the dungeons of Hell.

───────────────

9. Qur'an, 32:7.

Also, it is established by inductive reasoning and the investigations of the sciences that man is the most exalted among animals and the most important. For he discovers with his reason the steps between the apparent causes and effects existent in the universe, and the relationships of causes, which follow on after each other in succession. And, in order to imitate Divine art and orderly and wise dominical creation with his own insignificant art, and in order to understand Divine actions and Divine art through his partial knowledge and his own arts, he has been given the faculty of will as a scale and measure. Thus, the fact that man knows the universal, all-embracing actions and attributes of the All-Glorious Creator through the materials he works through the exercise of his will proves that he is the most honoured and exalted creature in the universe.

Also, according to the testimony of the truths of Islam concerning man and the universe, the most noble and exalted, the most excellent and the highest, are the people of Islam, who are the people of truth and reality. And, according to inductive reasoning and the testimony of history, among the people of truth, the most exalted among honoured mankind, the most excellent and superior was the Prophet Muhammad (PBUH). This is testified to by his thousand miracles, his elevated morals, and the truths of Islam and the Qur'an.

Since the three truths of this half argument give such news, is it at all possible that mankind should refute the testimony of so many sciences and deny this reasoning with their depravity, and, being perversely obstinate in the face of Divine will and pre-eternal wisdom, which embraces the whole universe, continue in their iniquitous savagery, wilful godlessness and fearful destruction? Is it at all possible that they should continue in this way against Islam?

I swear with all my strength and, if I possessed them, with innumerable tongues by the All-Wise and Glorious One, the All-Beauteous Maker, Who creates the world with this perfect order, and the universe, from particles to the planets, from a fly's wing to the lamps in the heavens, with an unbounded wisdom of regularity, that it is in no way possible for mankind, contrary to every other sort of being and opposed to the other species, which are its small brothers, to stand in opposition to the order in the universe through its universal acts of evil and to eat and digest the bitter fruits which, for thousands of years, have been the cause of evil predominating over good among men.

This possibility could only occur by supposing the impossible, that, although man is at the degree of having been charged with the 'supreme trust' over the universe, has the rank of Divine vicegerent of the earth, and is an elevated elder brother to the other beings in the universe, he was the lowest, most base, most wretched, most harmful and most insignificant, and as a consequence had stealthily entered the universe and caused chaos in it. This impossibility can in no way be accepted.

This half argument of mine for this fact leads to this conclusion that just as the existence of Heaven and Hell in the hereafter is a necessary fact, so too shall the religion of good and truth prevail absolutely in the future so that, as is the case with all other beings, good and virtue will prevail absolutely over mankind; and mankind may be equal to the rest of their brothers in the universe; and it may be said that the mystery of pre-eternal wisdom is established in mankind also.

In Short : As the definite facts mentioned above demonstrate, the choice result of the universe and the most important creature in the view of the Creator is man. And as man's wrongful conduct up to this time necessitates the existence of Hell, so do his comprehensive innate abilities and potentialities and the truths of his belief related to the universe self-evidently necessitate Paradise. Thus, since he cannot endure the crimes, and two world wars, which have made the cosmos weep, and cannot digest the bitter evils he has swallowed; and because of his conduct, at which he is sick and through which he has filthied the whole face of the earth; and since he has caused humanity to fall to the most abject level and cannot endure the crime of having overturned a thousand years of progress; most certainly and without any doubt, if some ghastly catastrophe does not soon break loose over his head, the truths of Islam will be the means of delivering man from the low and debased degree to which he has fallen, of cleansing the face of the earth, and securing universal peace. We beseech this from the mercy of the All-Merciful and Compassionate One, and we await it with hope.

Second Word

The Second Word has been born in my thought as a result of my experiences in the course of life. It is as follows:

Despair is a most grievous sickness and it has entered the heart of the world of Islam. It is despair that has as though killed us so that a small state of one or two million in the West has as though made twenty million Muslims in the East its servants and their country, its colony. And it is despair that has killed our high morals, and causing us to abandon the public good, has restricted our sight to personal benefits.

It is despair too that has destroyed our morale. Although with little power we were victorious from east to west through the moral strength that arose from belief, because it was destroyed through despair, tyrannical foreigners have made three hundred million Muslims their captives for the last four hundred years.

And because of this despair, Muslims even suppose the indifference and despondency of others to be an excuse for their own laziness and say: "What is it to me?" Saying, "Everybody is contemptible, like me," they abandon the courageousness of belief and fail to perform their Islamic duties.

Since the sickness of despair has inflicted so much tyranny on us and is killing us, we shall totally shatter it with the verse,

Do not despair of God's mercy.[10]

God willing, we shall destroy it with the truth of the Hadith, "Even if a thing is not wholly obtained, it should not be wholly left."

Despair is a most grievous sickness of communities and nations, a cancer. It is an obstacle to achievement and is opposed to the truth of the Sacred Hadith, "I am with my bondsman who thinks favourably of Me." It is the quality and pretext of cowards, the base and the impotent. It does not tell of Islamic courage. It cannot be the quality of a people like the Arabs in particular, who among mankind have been privileged with a fine character that is the cause of pride. The nations of the Islamic world have

---

10. Qur'an, 39:53.

taken lessons from the Arabs' fortitude. God willing, once more the Arabs will give up despair and will stand together with the Turks, who are the heroic army of Islam, and will unfurl the banner of the Qur'an in every part of the world.

Third Word

This Third Word I have learnt from the studies and researches I have carried out in the course of my life and from my experience of the ups and downs of social life; its summary and essence are as follows: truthfulness is the basis and foundation of Islam, and the bond between people of good character, and the basis of elevated emotions. Since this is so, as the foundation of the life of our society, we must bring to life truthfulness and honesty, and cure our moral and spiritual sicknesses with them.

Yes, truthfulness and honesty are the vital principles in the life of Islamic society. Hypocrisy is a sort of actualized lying. Flattery and artifice are cowardly lying. Duplicity and double-dealing are harmful lying. And as for lying, it is to slander the All-Glorious Maker's power.

Unbelief in all its varieties is falsehood and lying. Belief is truthfulness and honesty. As a consequence of this, there is a limitless distance between truth and falsehood; they should be as distant from one another as the East is from the West. Like fire and light, they should not become mixed with one another. However, cruel politics and tyrannical propaganda have mixed and confused them, and have also thrown into confusion man's achievements.[11]

Truthfulness and lying are as distant from one another as are belief and unbelief. With Muhammad's rising to the highest of the high by means of truthfulness in the Era of Bliss, and with the treasury of the truths of belief and the truths of the universe being unlocked with the key of truthfulness, truthfulness became the most valuable merchandise in the market of human society, and the goods most in demand.

Because of lying, the likes of Musaylima the Liar fell to the lowest of the low. Since that mighty revolution showed that at that time lying and falsehood were the key

---

11. O my brothers! It may be thought from this lesson of the Old Said that he was excessively concerned with politics and the social matters of Islam. But be careful, do not suppose he had taken the way of making religion a tool or means of politics. God forbid! With all his strength, he was making politics the tool of religion. He used to say: "I prefer one truth of religion to a thousand matters of politics. Indeed, he perceived at that time forty to fifty years ago that certain two-faced atheists were attempting to make politics the tool of irreligion, and in response to those aims and ideas of theirs, he tried to make politics a servant and tool of Islam and its truths.

However, twenty years later he saw that, in response to those clandestine double-dealing atheists' efforts to make politics the tool of irreligion, which they were doing under the pretext of westernization, a number of religious politicians were trying to make religion the tool of Islamic politics. But the sun of Islam cannot follow and be the tool of lights on the ground. And to make Islam a tool is to reduce its value and is a great crime. The Old Said even saw a pious scholar who, as a result of that sort of partisan politics, was enthusiastically praising a dissembler who agreed with his own political leanings, while criticizing and declaring to be deviant an upright teacher who opposed them. The Old Said said to him: "Should a devil support your political ideas, you would interpret it as mercy, and if an angel were to oppose them, you would curse him." As a result of this, the Old Said declared: "I seek refuge with God from Satan and politics," and for thirty-five years has given up politics.[12]

Signed: *Said Nursi*

12. Since the New Said gave up politics completely and did not follow them at all, the Turkish translation of the Damascus Sermon, a lesson of the Old Said which touches on politics, has been printed and made available.[13]

to blasphemies and superstition, they became one of the worst and filthiest goods on the market of the universe, and it was not as though everyone wanted to buy them, indeed, everyone detested them. Certainly the Companions, who were in the first line of that mighty revolution and in whose nature it was to buy things that were the cause of pride and to be customers for the most valuable goods and those most in demand, would never knowingly have advocated any falsehood. They would not have soiled themselves with lying. They would not have made themselves resemble Musaylima the Liar.

Indeed, since with all their strength and through innate disposition they were customers for truthfulness and honesty, which formed the steps whereby Muhammad (Upon whom be blessings and peace) rose to the highest of the high, and were the most sought-after merchandise and the most valuable commodity and the key to realities, and since as far as was possible they tried not to depart from truthfulness, it became an established principle in the science of Hadith and among scholars of the Shari'a that "the Companions always spoke the truth. Their narrations do not require to be investigated in the same way as other narrations. The Hadiths they related from the Prophet (PBUH) are all sound." A decisive argument for the consensus of the scholars of Hadith and the Shari'a is this fact.

---

13. Furthermore, although the twenty-seven years of the New Said's life together with the hundred and thirty sections of his writings and letters have been minutely examined by three courts (now one thousand courts) and by government officials; and although he was compelled to oppose the evil-doing apostates and double-dealers who were working against him; and although the order had even been given secretly for his execution; the fact that they were unable to find even the slightest indication suggesting that he had exploited religion for political ends proves decisively that he had not done so. We students of the Risale-i Nur are in wonder at this extraordinary situation and consider it to be a sign of the true sincerity that exists within the sphere of the Risale-i Nur.

Signed: *Students of the Risale-i Nur*

hus, at the time of the mighty revolution in the Era of Bliss truthfulness and lying were as far from one another as belief and unbelief, yet with the passing of time they have gradually drawn closer to each other. Political propaganda has sometimes given greater currency to lies, and evil and lying have to some degree taken the stage. It is because of this fact that no one could attain to the level of the Companions. Since this has been discussed in the Addendum to the Twenty-Seventh Word, which is about the Companions, we refer you to that and cut short the matter here.

O my brothers here in this Umayyad Mosque! And O my brothers who, forty to fifty years later, form the four hundred million believers in the vast mosque of the world of Islam! Salvation is only to be found through truthfulness and honesty. The *"support most unfailing"*[14] is honesty. That is to say, the strongest chain with which to be bound to salvation is honesty.

However, sometimes in the past lying abrogated this if there were advantages to be gained. Some scholars issued 'temporary' *fatwas* in case of necessity or for benefit. But in this age, such *fatwas* may not be given. For it has been abused so much that there may be only one benefit among a hundred harms. The judgement cannot therefore be based on benefit.

For example, the cause for shortening the ritual prayers while on a journey is hardship. But it cannot be the reason. For it has no determined limit and may be abused. The reason may only be the journey. Similarly, benefit may not be the reason for telling a lie. Because it has no specified limit and is a swamp breeding abuse. The judgement for a *fatwa* may not be based on it. In which

---

14. Qur'an, 2:256.

case, "Either truthfulness or silence." That is, there are two ways, not three; that is, not either the truth, or lies, or silence.

Since public order and security have been overturned through mankind's evident and ghastly lying and wilful misrepresentations, and through its abuse of benefits, mankind is clearly commanded and compelled to close the third way. Otherwise, the world wars, hideous revolutions, and decline and destruction that humanity has suffered in the past half-century will bring down some overwhelming disaster on men's heads.

Indeed, everything you say must be true, but it is not right to say everything true. If on occasion it is damaging, then be silent. But there is no *fatwa* for lying. Everything you say must be the truth, but you do not have the right to say everything that is true. Because if it is not sincere, it will have a detrimental effect and truth will be spent on wrong.

Fourth Word

What I am certain of from my experience of social life and have learnt from my life-time of study is the following:

The thing most worthy of love is love, and that most deserving of enmity is enmity. That is, love and loving, which render man's social life secure and lead to happiness are most worthy of love and being loved. Enmity and hostility are ugly and damaging, have overturned man's social life, and more than anything deserve loathing and enmity and to be shunned. Since this truth has been clearly explained in the Twenty-Second Letter of the Risale-i Nur, here we shall point it out only briefly. It is as follows:

The time for enmity and hostility has finished. Two world wars have shown how evil, destructive, and what an awesome wrong is enmity. It has become clear that there is no benefit in it at all. In which case, on condition they are not aggressive, do not let the evils of our enemies attract your enmity. Hell and Divine punishment are enough for them.

Sometimes, man's arrogance and self-worship cause him to be unjustly hostile towards believers without his being aware of it; he supposes himself to be right. But this hostility and enmity is to slight powerful causes of love towards the believers, like belief, Islam, and fellow-humanity; it is to reduce their value. It is a lunacy like preferring the insignificant causes of enmity to the causes of love, which are as great as a mountain.

Since love and enmity are contrary to one another, like light and darkness, they cannot truly combine. The opposite of whichever is predominant in the heart cannot at the same time be truly present. For example, if love is truly present, then enmity will be transformed into pity and compassion. This is the position towards the believers. Or if enmity is truly present in the heart, then love takes on the form of feigned approval, not interfering, and being apparently friendly. This may be the position towards unaggressive people of misguidance.

Indeed, the causes of love, like belief, Islam, humanity and fellow-feeling, are strong and luminous chains and immaterial fortresses. One sort of the causes of enmity towards the believers are personal matters, which are like small stones. In which case, to nourish true enmity towards a Muslim is a great error; it is like scorning the causes of love, which are as immense as a mountain.

In Short: Love, brotherhood, and affection are basic to Islam, and are its bond. The people of enmity resemble a spoilt child who wants to cry. He looks for an excuse, and something as insignificant as a fly's wing becomes the pretext. They resemble too an unfair, pessimistic person who so long as it is possible to distrust, never thinks favourably. He ignores ten good deeds due to one bad deed. Fairness and favourable thinking, which mark the Islamic character, reject this.

Fifth Word

The lesson I have learnt from the mutual consultation enjoined by the Shari'a is this: in this age, the single sin of one person does not remain as one; it sometimes swells, spreads and becomes a hundred sins. And sometimes a single good deed does not remain as one, but progresses to the order of thousands of good deeds. The reason for this is as follows:

Freedom in accordance with the Shari'a and the consultation enjoined by the Shari'a have demonstrated the sovereignty of our true nationhood. The foundation and spirit of our true nationhood is Islam. In so far as they have carried the standard of the Ottoman Caliphate and Turkish army in the name of that nationhood, the two true brothers of Arab and Turk are like the shell and citadel of the nationhood of Islam, and the sentries of that sacred citadel.

Thus, through the bond of this sacred nationhood, all the people of Islam become like a single tribe. Like the members of a tribe, the peoples and groups of Islam are bound and connected to one another through Islamic brotherhood. They assist one another morally, and if necessary, materially. It is as if all the groups of Islam are bound to each other with a luminous chain.

If a member of one tribe commits a crime, all its members are guilty in the eyes of another, enemy, tribe. It is as though each member of the tribe had committed the crime so that the enemy tribe becomes the enemy of all of them. That single crime becomes like thousands of crimes. While if a member of the tribe performs a good act that is the cause of pride affecting the heart of the tribe, all its members take pride in it. It is as if each person in the tribe feels proud at having done that good deed.

It is because of this fact that at this time, and particularly in forty to fifty years' time, evil and bad deeds will not remain with the perpetrator; they will transgress the rights of millions of Muslims. Numerous examples of this shall be seen in forty to fifty years' time.

O brothers who are listening to these words of mine here in the Umayyad Mosque! And O Muslim brothers in the mosque of the world of Islam forty to fifty years' later! Do not make apologies, saying: "We do no harm, but neither do we have the power to do anything beneficial; therefore we are excused." Such an apology is not acceptable. Your laziness and saying: "What is it to me?", and your displaying no effort and not getting into the working spirit through Islamic unity and true Islamic brotherhood, have done much damage and are an injustice to you.

Just as bad deeds thus mount to thousands, so also at this time good deeds, that is, good deeds that affect the sacredness of Islam, do not remain restricted to the one who performs them. Indeed, such good deeds may in fact be beneficial to millions of believers; they may strengthen the bonds of moral, spiritual, and material life. Therefore, this is not the time to cast oneself on the bed of idleness, saying: "What is it to me?"

O my brothers here in this mosque and my brothers forty to fifty years later in the mighty mosque of the world of Islam! Do not suppose I have mounted this place of delivering lessons in order to give you advice. I have done so to claim my rights from you. That is to say, the interests and happiness in this world and the hereafter of small groups are bound to masterly teachers like you, the Arabs and Turks, who are a vast and esteemed body. We, the Muslim groups who are your unhappy small brothers suffer harm through your idleness and laxity.

Especially the Arabs, who are esteemed, numerous, and either have been awakened or will be! First and foremost, I address you with these words. For you are our teachers and leaders, and the teachers and leaders of all the peoples of Islam, and you are the fighters of Islam. It was later that the mighty Turkish nation assisted you in that sacred duty.

Therefore, due to laziness your sin is great. Your good acts and deeds are also great and exalted. In particular we await with great expectation from Divine mercy the different Arab groups entering upon exalted circumstances in forty to fifty years' time, like those of the United States of America, and your being successful like in former times in establishing Islamic rule in half the globe, indeed, in most of it, which at the moment is in captivity.

If some fearful calamity does not soon erupt, the coming generation shall see it, God willing.

Beware, my brothers! Do not imagine that I am urging you with these words to busy yourselves with politics. God forbid! The truth of Islam is above all politics. All politics may serve it, but no politics can make Islam a tool for itself.

With my faulty understanding, I imagine Islamic society at this time in the form of a factory containing many machines. Should any components of the machines fall behind or encroach on another, which is its fellow, the machines cease to function. The exact time for Islamic unity is therefore beginning. It necessitates not paying attention to one another's personal faults.

I say this to you with regret and sadness that certain foreigners have taken our most valuable possessions and country from us and have given us a rotten price in return.

Similarly, they have taken from us our elevated morals and a part of our fine character that touches on social life, and they have made them the means of their progress. And it is their dissipated morals and dissipated character that they have given us as their price.

For example, because of the fine national feeling they have taken from us, one of them says: "Should I die, let my nation live, for I have an everlasting life in my nation." They have taken these words from us and it is the firmest foundation in their progress. These words proceed from the religion of truth and the truths of belief. They are our property, the property of the believers.

However, because of the obscene and bad character that infiltrated us from foreigners, a selfish man from

among us says: "If I die of thirst, let it not rain again any-
where in the world. If I do not experience happiness, let
the world go to rack and ruin as it wishes." These ridiculous words arise from lack of religion and from not recognizing the hereafter. They have entered among us from
outside and are poisoning us.

Also, because of the idea of nationhood which those
foreigners obtained from us, an individual becomes as
valuable as a nation. For a person's value is relative to his
endeavour. If a person's endeavour is his nation, that person forms a miniature nation on his own.

Because of the heedlessness of some of us and the foreigners' damaging characteristics that we have acquired,
and, despite our strong and sacred Islamic nationhood,
through everyone saying: "Me! Me!" and considering
personal benefits and not the nation's benefits, a thousand men have become like one man.

If a man's endeavour is limited to himself, he is not a
human being, for human beings are by nature civilized.
Man is compelled to consider his fellow humans. His personal life continues through social life. For example, how
many hands is he in need of to eat one load of bread, and
in return for it how many hands does he in effect kiss?
And how many factories is he connected to through the
clothes that he wears? You make the comparison! Since
he cannot survive with only skin like an animal, and is by
nature connected to his fellow humans, and is compelled
to pay them an immaterial price, by his nature, he main-
tains civilization. One who confines his view to his personal benefits abandons his humanity, and becomes an
iniquitous animal lacking all innocence. If nothing happens as a consequence and he has an authentic excuse,
that is an exception!

Sixth Word

T he key to Muslims' happiness in the life of Islamic society is the mutual consultation enjoined by the Shari'a. The verse,

Whose rule is consultation among themselves[15]

orders consultation as a fundamental principle. Just as the consultation of the ages and centuries that mankind has practised by means of history, a conjunction of ideas, formed the basis of man's progress and sciences, so too one reason for the backwardness of Asia, the largest continent, was the failure to practise that true consultation.

The key and discloser of the continent of Asia and its future is mutual consultation. That is to say, just as individuals should consult one another, so must nations and continents practise consultation. For it is the freedom that is in accordance with the Shari'a, which is born of the consultation enjoined by the Shari'a, and the noble-mindedness and compassion of belief that will loosen and remove the fetters and chains of the various forms of tyranny fastened to the feet of three hundred, rather, four hundred, million strong Islam. It is that lawful freedom which, adorned with the customs and observances of the Shari'a, will cast out the evils of dissolute Western civilization. The freedom born of the Shari'a, which arises from belief, enjoins two principles:

Belief necessitates not humiliating others through oppression and despotism and not degrading them, and

---

15. Qur'an, 42:38.

secondly, not abasing oneself before tyrants. Someone who is a true servant of God cannot be a slave to others. Do not make anyone other than God lord over your-selves. That is to say, someone who does not recognize God ascribes relative degrees of mastery to everything and everyone, and piles worries on his own head. For sure, the freedom born of the Shari'a is a bounty of Almighty God through the manifestation of His Names of All-Merciful and All-Compassionate; it is a characteristic of belief.

Long live truthfulness! Death to despair! Let love endure! Let mutual consultation find strength! Let those who follow their own whims and desires be the object of blame, reproach and detestation! And on those who fol-low right-guidance be peace and well-being! AMEN.

If it is asked: Why do you attach this much importance to mutual consultation? And how may the life and progress of mankind, in particular Asia, and particularly Islam, be achieved through mutual consultation?

We would answer: As is explained in the Twenty-First Flash of the Risale-i Nur, the Treatise on Sincerity, since just consultation results in sincerity and solidarity, three 'alifs'[16] become one hundred and eleven. Thus, three men between whom there is true solidarity may benefit the nation as much as a hundred men. Many historical events inform us that as a result of true sincerity, solidarity, and consultation, ten men may perform the work of a thou-sand.

Man's needs are endless and his enemies innumerable, his strength and capital insignificant, and the number of

---

16. *Alif:* the first letter of the Arabic alphabet, written with a single ver-ticle stroke: ' ['.

destructive, harmful humans who have become like monsters through lack of religion is increasing. In the face of those endless enemies and innumerable needs, man can continue his personal life only through the support and assistance proceeding from belief, and can maintain his social life only through the mutual consultation enjoined by the Shari'a, that again proceeds from the truths of belief. It is only thus that he can halt his enemies and open up a way to secure his needs.

* * *

First Addendum

A Summary of the Addendum to the Arabic Text of the Damascus Sermon

I n the Arabic addendum to the Damascus Sermon, the unassailable moral heroism born of belief in God was described by means of a truly subtle comparison. Here we shall set forth a summary of it and explain it.

Close to the beginning of the Second Constitutional Period (1908-1918), I joined Sultan Reşad's tour of Rumelia[1] on behalf of the Eastern Provinces. In our carriage of the train a discussion started with two friends who taught in the new secular schools and were well-versed in science. They asked me: "Which is more necessary and should be stronger, religious zeal or national zeal?" To which I replied:

With us Muslims religion and nationhood are united, although there is a theoretical, apparent and incidental

---

1. June, 1911. [Tr.]

difference between them. Indeed, religion is the life and spirit of the nation. When they are seen as different and separate from each other, religious zeal encompasses both the common people and upper classes, whereas national zeal is felt by one person out of a hundred, that is, a person who is ready to sacrifice his personal benefits for the nation. Since this is the case, religious zeal must be the basis with regard to the rights of all the people, while national zeal must serve it and be its fortress.

This is especially so since we people of the East are not like those of the West: our hearts are governed by the sense of religion. The fact that it was in the East that pre-eternal Divine Determining sent most of the prophets indicates that only the sense of religion will awaken the East and impel it to progress. A convincing argument for this is the era of the Prophet Muhammad (PBUH) and those who followed after him.

O my friends who are studying with me in this travelling school called a train! You asked me to which one should give more importance, religious zeal or national zeal. And now, all you who received secular education and are travelling with me towards the future in the train of time! I say the following to you as well:

Religious zeal and Islamic nationhood have completely fused in the Turks and Arabs, and may not now be separated. Islamic zeal is a luminous chain which is most strong and secure and is not born of this world. It is a support that is firm and certain, and will not fail. It is an unassailable fortress that cannot be razed.

When I said this to those two enlightened school teachers, they said to me: "What evidence is there for this? For a claim as great as this an equally great proof and powerful evidence are necessary. What is the evidence?"

Suddenly the train emerged from a tunnel. We put our heads out of the window and looked. We saw that a child not yet six years old was standing right next to the railway line where the train was about to pass. I said to my two teacher friends:

Look, this child is answering our question just by the way he is acting. Let the innocent child be the teacher in our travelling school instead of me. See, his behaviour is stating the following truth:

You can see that the child is standing only a metre's distance from where this hideous monster will pass the minute it roars shrieking out of its hole, the tunnel, with its fearful onslaught. Although it is roaring and threatening with its overwhelming attack saying: "Anything in my way better watch out!", the innocent child is standing right next to it. With perfect courage, heroism and freedom of spirit he gives no importance at all to its threats. He has contempt for the monster's onslaught, and says with his childish heroism: "Hey, railway train, you can't frighten me with your thunderous roars!"

It is as if he is saying too through his resolution and fortitude: "Hey, railway train, you're the prisoner of a system! Your bit and bridle are in the hands of the one who's driving you. It's beyond your power to attack me. You can't seize me and hold me under your despotism. Off with you! Get on your way! Carry on down the track at the command of your driver!'"

O friends in this train and brothers who are studying science fifty years later! Traversing time, suppose that with their proverbial heroism Rustam of Iran and Hercules of Greece are there in place of the innocent child. Since at their time there were no trains, of course there was not the belief that trains move regularly, according to a system. When the train suddenly roars out of its hole, the tunnel, snorting thunder and fire, with lightening in its eyes, how Rustam and Hercules rush to one side at its threatening onslaught! How those two heroes are terrified and flee! For all their proverbial courage they run more than a thousand metres.

So look, see how their freedom and courage dissolve in the face of the monster's threat. There is nothing they can do but flee. They do not realize that it is an obedient steed, because they do not believe in its driver and orderly system. They imagine it to be a sort of lion with twenty terrifying and rapacious lions the size of waggons attached to its rear.

O my brothers and my friends who are listening to these words after fifty years! What gives the five-year-old child greater freedom and courage than those two heroes, and a fearlessness and confidence far exceeding theirs, is faith, trust and belief. Belief in the order and system of the railway, which is a seed of truth in that innocent child's heart. Belief that the reins of the train are in the hands of a driver, that its movement is regulated, that someone is driving it on his own account.

While what terrifies the two heroes and makes their consciences prisoners to delusion is their ignorant lack of faith; it is the fact that they do not know the driver and do not believe in the order and system.

The heroism which arose from the innocent child's belief in the comparison is like the heroism of a number of tribes —in particular Turkish and Turkified tribes— from among the Islamic peoples who, by reason of the faith and belief that was rooted in their hearts, for a thousand years raised the banner of Islam and all its perfections in the face of more than a hundred nations and states in Asia, Africa and half Europe; who went to meet death laughing and saying: "If I die, I shall be a martyr; if I kill, I shall be a champion of Islam."

Foremost the Turks and Arabs, and all the Muslim peoples, never fearing, confronted with the heroism of belief the unending succession of hostile events in this world, and the threats of that fearsome railway train which is inimical to man's comprehensive disposition, from microbes, even, to comets. Through the submission to Divine Determining and Decree that arises from belief, they took lessons, and gained wisdom and a sort of worldly happiness in place of terror and fright. The fact that, like the innocent child, they displayed this extraordinary heroism demonstrates that in this world as in the hereafter the absolute ruler of the future will be the nation of Islam.

The cause of the truly strange fear, alarm and anxiety of those two strange heroes in the two comparisons was their lack of belief, their ignorance, and their misguidance; a truth which the Risale-i Nur demonstrates with hundreds of proofs. It is as follows:

Unbelief and misguidance show to the people of misguidance a universe consisting wholly of series of terrible enemies. Thousands of different enemies from the solar system to tubercular bacteria are attacking unfortunate humanity with the hands of blind force, aimless chance, and deaf nature.

By presenting to man's comprehensive disposition, and his endless needs and infinite desires, continuous fear, pain and anxiety, unbelief and misguidance are forms of Hell; it puts those who follow it into a sort of Hell while still in this world.

All science and human progress outside religion and

belief is worth nothing, like the heroism of Rustam and Hercules. All it does is to administer injections to deaden the senses so that through drunkenness and dissipation those grievous fears may be temporarily forgotten.

Thus, on the one hand belief and unbelief yield fruits and results in the hereafter like Paradise and Hell, and on the other in this world belief ensures a sort of Paradise, and transforms death into a release from duty, while unbelief makes this world into a sort of Hell, destroys true human happiness and reduces death to eternal noth-ingness. The Risale-i Nur, relying on definite insight and direct cognition, has demonstrated this truth with hun-dreds of proofs. Therefore, we refer you to those and cut short the discussion here.

If you wish to see the truth that lies in this comparison, raise your head and look at the universe. Look and see how many vehicles there are like the railway train: bal-loons, cars, aeroplanes, ships of the land and the sea... the globes of the stars, the heavenly bodies, the chains of events and successive occurrences that pre-eternal power creates with order, regularity, wisdom and purpose on land and sea and in space.

Anyone who has intelligence and sight is able to see most of these chains of events in the manifest world and corporeal universe and to confirm their existence. Sim-ilarly, they may confirm that there are even more wonder-ful successive events created by pre-eternal power in the spirit and incorporeal worlds.

Thus, all these material and immaterial chains of events in the universe attack, threaten and frighten the unbelieving people of misguidance; they destroy their moral and spiritual strength. Whereas, for the people of belief, rather than threatening and frightening them, they bring them joy and comfort, and give them hope and strength.

This is because the believers understand through their belief that an All-Wise Maker is impelling each of those innumerable chains of events, corporeal and incorporeal railway trains and travelling universes, to carry out their functions within a perfect orderliness, regularity, wisdom and purpose; that He is causing them to work. Not one jot are they confused in their duties, nor can they transgress against one another.

The believers see through their belief that these events are displaying the perfections of His art and the manifestations of His Beauty in the universe. Thus belief gives all moral strength to them and demonstrates a sample of eternal happiness.

Nothing, then, no science, no human progress, can ensure moral strength in the face of the ghastly pains and fears that arise from the people of misguidance's unbelief, nor give them any comfort. They destroy their courage, but temporarily draw a veil of neglect over them, deceiving them.

The believers, by reason of their belief, look on these events, not with fear and crumbled moral strength but with an extraordinary strength and fortitude, and with the truth that is in belief, like the innocent child in the comparison. They observe the planning and will of an All-Wise Maker within the sphere of His wisdom and are saved from delusion and fears.

They understand and say: "If it were not for the command and permission of the All-Wise Maker, these travelling universes could not be in motion, they could do nothing." With perfect confidence, they manifest happiness in the life of this world, each according to his degree.

When the seed of truth born of belief and true religion are not present in a person's heart and conscience, and are not his point of support, in the same way that Rustam and Hercules' courage and heroism crumbled in the comparison, such a person's courage and morale too will be annihilated and his conscience will decay. He will become prisoner to all the events in the universe. He will sink to being a trembling beggar before everything.

Since the Risale-i Nur has demonstrated this truth concerning belief and the fearsome wretchedness that misguidance brings in this world with hundreds of decisive proofs, we shall cut short this long and extensive truth here.

Man in this century has perceived that his greatest need is for moral and spiritual strength, solace, and fortitude. Therefore, for him to abandon Islam and the truths of belief at this time, which are a point of support and secure the moral strength, solace, and happiness he needs, and, instead of benefiting from Islamic nationhood, under the pretext of becoming westernized, for him to rely on misguidance, dissipation, and lying politics and diplomacy, which completely destroy and annihilate all moral strength, solace, and fortitude, are acts far from all benefit and profit for mankind. Just how far they are from benefiting mankind, foremost the Islamic world, and all mankind, will realize. They will be awakened to this truth, and, if time has not run out for this world, they will adhere to the truths of the Qur'an.

*   *   *

First Addendum
Second Part

As in the comparison above, in the former period at the beginning of the Second Constitutional Period, a number of religiously-minded deputies said to the Old Said:

"You make politics the tool of religion and the Shari'a in every way possible and make it serve religion. You only support freedom on account of the Shari'a. And you favour constitutionalism in so far as it is in conformity with the Shari'a. That means one cannot have freedom and constitutionalism without the Shari'a. It is for this reason that they included you among those who said 'We want the Shari'a' during the Thirty-First of March Incident."

The Old Said told them: "Yes, it is only through the truths of Islam that the Islam will prosper and flourish. Islamic society can function only through the Shari'a of Islam and its worldly happiness be achieved. Otherwise justice will disappear, public security be overturned, immorality and base qualities prevail, and everything be run by liars and sycophants. As a small proof out of thousands of this truth, I offer the following story for your attention:

One time in the desert, a man was the guest of a nomad who was one of the people of reality. He saw that the desert-dwellers did not concern themselves with guarding their belongings. His host had even left some money openly in the corner of the room. The guest asked him:

"Aren't you frightened of thieves, just throwing your belongings in the corner like that?"

His host answered: "We do not have any thieves here."

The guest said: "We put our money in safes and lock them, but it is still frequently stolen."

His host told him: "We cut off the hands of thieves as a Divine command and on account of the justice of the Shari'a."

Whereupon the guest exclaimed: "Then most of you must be lacking a hand!"

His host told him: "I am fifty years old, and yet in my whole life I have only seen one person with their hand cut off."

The guest was ashamed and said: "Although everyday in my country we put fifty people in prison for theft, it does not have one hundredth of the effectiveness of your justice here."

The host said: "You have been unmindful of an important truth and have ignored a strange and powerful fact, as a result of which true justice has escaped you. In place of general good, under an apparent justice, hatred and vicious and partisan currents intervene, destroying the effect of the judgements. The truth is as follows:

With us, the moment a thief stretches out his hand to seize another's property, he recalls the punishment of the Shari'a. The command revealed from the Divine Throne comes to his mind. Through the sense of belief and ear of the heart, he as though hears the verse:

> As to the thief, male or female, cut off his or her hands,[1]

which calls for "the execution of the thief's hand," and his belief and elevated emotions are stirred into action. From around his spirit and the depths of his conscience a state of mind is given rise to which as though attacks the inclination to steal. The inclination, which arises from the instinctual soul and lust, is stifled and recedes; by degrees it is completely extinguished. For not only the mind and imagination, but also the inner faculties, the intellect, heart, and conscience, together attack that desire and emotion. By recalling the punishment of the Shari'a the thief's conscience restrains and prohibits him, confronting that desire and silencing it.

Yes, belief places in the heart and mind a permanent 'prohibitor;' when sinful desires emerge from the soul, it repulses them, declaring: "it is forbidden!"

Man's actions result from the inclinations of his heart and emotions. They come from the sensibilities of the spirit and its needs. The spirit is stirred into action through the light of belief. If an act is good, he does it; if it is evil, he tries to restrain himself. Blinder emotions will not drive him down the wrong road and defeat him.

In Short: When the punishments are carried out in the name of the Divine commands and dominical justice, both the spirit, and the intellect, and the conscience, and

---

1. Qur'an, 5:38.

man's innate subtle faculties are affected and influenced. It is for this reason that the execution of a punishment once in fifty years is more effective than your imprisoning numerous people every day. Your penalties affect only your imaginations, for when one of you decides to steal something, suffering a penalty on account the country and nation and its benefits seems imaginary; or he thinks others will condemn him if they know about it; or it occurs to him that if it turns out unfavourably the government will send him to prison. So only his power of imagination feels minor discomfort. And the powerful desire issuing from his instinctual soul and emotions — particularly if he is needy as well— will overpower him. Then the penalty will be ineffective in making him refrain from committing the bad deed. Anyway, because they are not a Divine command, the penalties are not justice. They are vain and futile like performing the prayers without taking ablutions and not facing the *qibla*. That is to say, true justice and effective penalties are those which are in accordance with the Divine command and executed in its name. Others can have only a minimal effect.

Other universal and all-embracing Divine injunctions may be compared with this small question of theft, so that it may be understood that man's happiness and well-being in this world are possible only through justice. As for justice, it can be achieved only through direct application of the way shown by the Qur'an.

(This marks the end of the summary of the story)

* * *

It was imparted to my heart that if mankind does not come swiftly to its senses and open courts in the name of

Divine justice and in accordance with the truths of Islam, calamities both material and non-material will break over men's heads and they will surrender to anarchy and lawlessness.

The Old Said related the above story to some religious deputies of that time, and it was included forty-five years ago in the Addendum to the Damascus Sermon.

Now, since the story and previous comparison are instruction relevant to the present time rather than that time, we offer it to the deputies who sincerely support religion so they may take note of it.

S a i d   N u r s i

*   *   *

---

2. Because we do not know Arabic, we requested of Ustad that he should teach us concerning his Arabic treatise which was published under the title of The Damascus Sermon (*Hutbe-i Şamiye*). He did so for several days and we wrote down what he said. He used to repeat some of the things he taught so that they would stick in our minds. We found the story and comparison at the end useful in explaining the question. And the reason we have offered them first of all for the attention of members of universities and deputies who support religion is because when Ustad [Bediuzzaman Said Nursi] began to explain this subject, he said: "I put you in the place of the two teachers from the modern schools in the railway train, and the sincerely religious deputies of the present time in the place of the deputies of forty-five years ago who asked the question about the Shari'a." If they wish we can show them all our notes about the Damascus Sermon, and if needed, we can publish them.

We wanted Ustad to teach us about the politics of the Islamic world. But since he had given up politics thirty-five years previously, he explained to us instead this translation of the Damascus Sermon of the Old Said, which touches on Islamic politics. It is a lesson on account of the Old Said.

Signed: His students, *Tahiri, Zübeyr, Bayram, Ceylan, Sungur, Abdullah, Ziya, Sadık, Hüsnü, Hamza*

First Addendum
Third Part

[This part of the Addendum consists of newspaper articles written by Bediuzzaman Said Nursi forty-two years ago.]

Long Live the Illustrious Shari'a!

Volkan No: 73
21 Safer 1327/ 1 Mart 1325/ 14 March 1909

Deputies of the Assembly!

I am going to write a single sentence, which though very long, is extremely succinct. Take note of it, for in its prolixity is conciseness. It is this:

If you apply the title of the ILLUSTRIOUS SHARI'A to the justice, mutual consultation, and restriction of power to the law which is the Constitution and constitutionalism, and make it the authority for your rulings and apply its principles, what will you lose? For it is the true and rightful owner of this glorious, effective title and comprises the following manifold benefits: it is the source of absolute justice; provides us with a sure point of support; establishes constitutionalism on a firm base; saves the doubtful and anxious from the abyss of their bewilderment; guarantees our future in this world and our lives in the next; delivers 'Divine rights,' that is, the rights of the public, from wrongful exploitation; preserves our national life; attracts all minds and demonstrates to westerners our constancy, maturity, and existence; saves you from being called to account in this world and the next; establishes unanimity of purpose and result; gives rise to public opinion, the spirit of consensus; prohibits the corrupt evils of civilization from entering the bounds of freedom and our civilization; delivers us from begging to Europe; through the mystery of miraculousness, in a short space of time makes us traverse the long distance in progress that we have lagged behind; gains great value for us by in a short time uniting Arab, Turk, Persian, and Semite; shows the collective personality of the government to be Muslim; by preserving the spirit of the Constitution and Article Eleven,[1] saves you from perjuring yourselves; gives the lie to Europe's old false ideas about us; makes it affirmed that Muhammad (Upon whom be blessings and peace) is the Seal of the Prophets and the Shari'a is eternal; forms a barrier against irreligion, the destroyer of civilization; with its shining face, puts an end to the darkness of the conflict and confusion of ideas; unites all the religious scholars and preachers and causes them to assist the nation's happiness, and makes the government and its activities serve licit constitutionalism; since its absolute justice is compassionate, reconciles and binds to a greater

---

1. Article 11 of the Constitution: "Every Ottoman is free to practise his religion on condition only that no breach of public order or good morals is committed." [Tr.]

extent the non-Muslim minorities; inspires the most pusillanimous man with true feelings of progress, self-sacrifice, and patriotism the same as the bravest, and the most common man the same as the most elevated; delivers us from vice, wastefulness, and inessential needs, all of which destroy civilization; gives a spur to endeavour by developing this world as well as saving the hereafter; teaches the principles of good morals and elevated emotions, the life of civilization; acquits each of you deputies from fifty thousand people claiming their rights from you; shows you to be a small, licit sample of the consensus of the Umma; because of pure intention makes all your actions into worship; and saves you from criminal conspiracy against the spiritual lives of three hundred million Muslims; —since it comprises this many benefits, what will you lose if you apply the title of the Shari'a to constitutionalism?

Long live the Illustrious Shari'a!

Said Nursi

* * *

Long Live the Shari'a of Muhammad!
(Upon whom be blessings and peace)

Volkan No. 77
25 Safar 1327/ 5 Mart 1325/ 18 March 1909

Since the Illustrious Shari'a proceeds from pre-eternal Divine speech, it will continue for all eternity. Our salvation from the vile tyranny of the evil-commanding soul is through reliance on Islam, by holding fast to that 'rope most strong.' We may profit thoroughly from true freedom by seeking help from belief. For one who is truly a slave and servant of the world's Maker will not stoop to worshipping His creatures. Everyone is a commander in his own world and is therefore charged with the 'greater *jihad*' in it, with assuming the morality of Muhammad (Upon whom be blessings and peace), and raising to life his practices.

Rulers of this land! If you want success, conform to the Divine laws! Otherwise you will be unsuccessful. For the fact that all the known prophets appeared in the lands of Islam and the Ottomans is a sign of Divine Determining that the steam of the engine of the progress of this country's people is religion. The flowers of these fields of Asia, Afica, and Rumelia will grow and flourish through the light of Islam.

Religion may not be sacrificed for the sake of this world. At one time the matters of the Shari'a were given as the bribe to preserve the now defunct despotism. Did anything other than harm result from giving up and sacrificing the matters of religion? This nation's heart disease is weakness in religion; it will regain its health through strengthening it.

The way of our society is love for love and enmity towards enmity. That is, assisting love between Muslims and routing the soldiers of hostility.

Our way is also to adopt the morality of Muhammad (Upon whom be blessings and peace) and revive his practices. Our guide is the Illustrious Shari'a, our sword its decisive proofs, and our aim to uphold the Word of God. All believers are in meaning members of our society, while formal membership is by making determined effort to raise to life in one's own world the Prophet's practices. First of all, in the name of the Shari'a, we call on the religious scholars, shaykhs, and students of the religious schools, who are the guides of the general public, to unite.

Said Nursi

* * *

A Warning

With two false comparisons, journalists, the public orators, have plunged this nation into a bog.

The First is by comparing the provinces with Istanbul. But if philosophy is taught to children who cannot yet read, what is taught will be superficial...

The Second: They have compared Istanbul to Europe. But if a man dresses in a garment deemed suitable to women, he becomes ridiculous and the object of scorn.

Said Nursi

* * *

Reality

Volkan No: 70
18 Safar 1327/ 26 Şubat 1324/ 11 March 1909

We have been members of the *İttihad-ı Muhammedî* (The Muhammadan Union) (Upon whom be blessings and peace) since man undertook the trust in pre-eternity.[2] The reason for our unity is Divine Unity; our oath and pledge is belief; we are united because we affirm Divine Unity. All believers are charged with upholding the Word of God, and at this time the most effective means of doing this is material progress. For the Europeans are crushing us under their tyranny with the weapons of science and industry. We shall therefore wage *jihad* with the weapons of science and industry on ignorance, poverty, and conflicting ideas, the worst enemies of upholding the Word of God.

As for external *jihad*, we shall refer it to the decisive proofs of the Illustrious Shari'a. For conquering the civilized is through persuasion, not through force as though they were savages who understand nothing. We are devotees of love, we do not have time for enmity. Republicanism[3] consists of justice, mutual consultation, and the restriction of power to the law. The Illustrious Shari'a was founded thirteen centuries ago, so to go begging to Europe in the question of laws is a great crime towards

---

2. "*Qālū balā.*" See, Qur'an, 7:172. [Tr.]
3. At that time it was 'constitutionalism,' now it is 'republicanism.'

the religion of Islam. It is like facing the north while praying. Power must reside in the law, otherwise arbitrary rule spreads. The saying "It is Allah Who is the Strong, the Most Firm" must govern the conscience. That is possible through general education and widespread civilization, or in the name of the religion of Islam. Otherwise absolutism will always prevail.

Unity may be achieved through Divine Guidance, not through personal whims and desires.

People are free, but they are still slaves of God. Everything is free now; the Shari'a is free, constitutionalism is free. We shall not give the matters of the Shari'a as a bribe. One may not make the faults of others the basis of and excuse for one's own faults.

Despair is an obstacle to all achievement. The saying: "What is it to me, let other's think" is a souvenir of absolutism. I do not know what should be interposed to tie together these sentences since I do not know Turkish, and leave it for the readers to work it out.

Said Nursi

* * *

The Voice of Truth

Volkan No: 86
5 Rebîülevvel 1327/ 14 Mart 1325/ 27 March 1909

The way of Muhammad (Upon whom be blessings and peace) is free of all doubts and trickery, and therefore does not condescend to concealing things, which is suggestive of doubt and trickery. Anyway, such a mighty, extensive, all-embracing truth could in no way be hidden, especially from the people of this time. How could an ocean be concealed in a pitcher?

I repeat: the means of unity of the *İttihad-ı Muhammedî* (Muhammadan Union), which in reality is Islamic Unity, is Divine Unity. Its oath and pledge is belief. Its associations and councils are the mosques, religious schools, and Sufi meeting-places. Its membership consists of all believers. It code of rules are the practices of the Prophet (PBUH). Its laws are the commands and prohibitions of the Shari'a. This Union consists not of numbers but of worship.

Fear and causing fear are both hypocrisy, but there is no hypocrisy in performing the obligatory acts of religion. The obligatory act of greatest importance at the present time is Islamic Unity. While the aim and goal of Unity [or the Muhammadan Union] is to stir into life the long, many-branched, far-reaching luminous chain which binds together the centres of Islam and their places of worship, to arouse those bound to it, and through the wishes and promptings of their consciences drive them to the way of progress.

The way of this Union is love; its enmity is only for ignorance, poverty, and strife. Non-Muslims should feel sure that this Union attacks only those three facts. Our actions towards non-Muslims consist only of persuasion, for we know them to be civilized. And we suppose them to be fair-minded, so we should demonstrate that Islam is lovable and elevated. The lax and negligent should know that they cannot ingratiate themselves with the Europeans by being irreligious, for they only show that they are unprincipled. And no one likes unprincipledness and anarchy. Those who join this Union after due investigation, will not leave it by blindly imitating such people. We present to public opinion the ideas, way, and reality of the Muhammadan Union, which is Islamic Unity. If anyone has any objections, let him voice them; we are ready to answer them.

All the lions of the world are bound to this chain;
Could the fox chew through it by trickery?

Said Nursi

* * *

A part I left out of the Programme of My Aims, which I published[4]

One channel of modern education, which flows in from outside, should consist of some of the members of the religious schools, so that it may be purified of rancour and hatred. For coming from another channel it is polluted and cloudy. It has had a negative effect on some minds oppressed by the tyranny which arises from the swamp of idleness and breathes through the poison of despotism; it must therefore pass through the filter of the Shari'a. It will be transformed through the efforts of the religious scholars.

Peace on those who follow right-guidance.

S a i d   N u r s i

* * *

---

4. See, Volkan, Nos: 83, 84. [Tr.]

To Dispel Any Fears

Volkan No: 90
9 Rebîülevvel 1327/ 18 Mart 1325/ 31 March 1909

I shall reply to nine groundless fears voiced about the *İttihad-ı Muhammedî* (Muhammadan Union).

First Groundless Fear: It is inappropriate to put forward the question of religion at a sensitive time such as the present.

The Answer: We love religion, and we love this world for the sake of religion. "There is no good in this world without religion."

Secondly: Since in constitutionalism sovereignity belongs to the nation, the nation's existence has to be demonstrated, and our nation is only Islam. For the strongest bond of Arab, Turk, Kurd, Albanian, Circassian, and Laz, and their firmest nationhood, is nothing other than Islam. The foundations of an array of states are being laid, due to negligence and strife incited through the revival of the partisanship and tribalism of the Age of Ignorance, which died one thousand three hundred years ago. We have seen this.

Second Groundless Fear: By using this name specifically you make non-members feel alarm and anxiety?

The Answer: I have explained this before, but because

it has not been read or has been misunderstood, I am obliged to repeat it. It is like this:

What is meant when we say the *İttihad-ı Muhammedî* (Muhammad Union), which is Islamic Unity, is the unity between all believers, whether potential or actual. It does not refer to the society in Istanbul and Anatolia. A single drop of water is still water. The word cannot be thought of as specific. Its true definition is as follows:

Its foundations stretch from east to west and from north to south; its centre are the holy places of Mecca and Medina; its point of unity is Divine Unity; its oath and pledge is belief; its code of regulations, the practices of the Prophet (PBUH); its code of laws, the commands and prohibitions of the Shari'a; its clubs and councils, all the religious schools, mosques, and Sufi meeting-houses; the society's eternal press organ are all Islamic books, and its constant one is foremost the Qur'an and all Qur'anic commentaries (and at this time, the Risale-i Nur, which is a Qur'anic commentary), as well as all moderate religious papers and journals whose aim is to uphold the Word of God; its membership consists of all believers; and its leader is the Glory of the World (PBUH).

What we want now is the awakening and attention of believers, for the effect of public attention is undeniable. The aim of the Union and its purpose is to uphold the Word of God, and its way is to wage the 'greater *jihad*' with one's own soul, and to guide others. Ninety-nine per cent of the endeavours of this blessed society are not political. They are rather turned towards good morals and moderation, which are the opposite of politics, and other lawful aims. For very few societies have adopted this as their function, although its value and importance is immense. Only one out of a hundred of its members will be connected with politics by way of offering guidance to politicians. Their swords are decisive proofs. And just as their way is love, so will they encourage the love included in the seed of the brotherhood between believers to grow, like a tree of Tuba.

Fifth Groundless Fear: Is there not the possibility that the Europeans will be perturbed by it?

The Answer: Those who consider this to be a possibility are themselves perturbed. For it is refuted by the Europeans praising Islam in lectures[5] and describing its elevatedness, in the very centres of their bigotry. Also, it is not they who are our enemies; what has in reality brought us this low is opposition to the Shari'a, which is the result of ignorance, thus preventing us from upholding the Word of God; and poverty and its fruits of immorality and bad conduct; and conflict and its products of strife and hatred; the attacks of our Union are directed at these three enemies.

In the Middle Ages, Islam was compelled to be bigoted and hostile in the face of the Europeans' savagery, but it nevertheless maintained its justice and moderation. It never instituted inquisitions and such like. In this time of modern civilization, the Europeans are civilized and powerful, and harmful hostility and bigotry have therefore disappeared. For in respect of religion, the civilized are to be conquered through persuasion, not through force, and through showing by conforming to its commands in actions and conduct that Islam is elevated and lovable. Force and enmity are only to combat the barbarity of savages.

Sixth Groundless Fear: Some people say

---

5. This alludes to lectures given by Bismarck, Carlyle, and others.

that Islamic Unity, which aims to implement the practices of the Prophet (PBUH), limits freedom and is opposed to the requirements of civilization.

The Answer: The true believer is truly free. One who is the slave and servant of the Maker of the world will not condescend to lower himself before His creatures. That is to say, freedom is increased to the degree belief is strengthened.

Absolute freedom, however, is absolute savagery; indeed, it is animality. From the point of view of humanity, too, freedom has to be restricted.

Secondly: Some lax and dissolute individuals want not to be free, but to be the vile slaves of their evil-commanding souls.

In Short: The freedom outside the bounds of the Shari'a is either despotism, or slavery to the soul, or animality, or savagery. The heedless and atheists who want such freedom should know that they will never make any European with a conscience love them through vice and irreligion, nor will they resemble them. For no one loves the dissolute and the unprincipled. And if a man wears a woman's dress, he merely becomes ridiculous.

Seventh Groundless Fear: The Muhammadan Union has split away from the other religious groups, and this leads to rivalry and mutual aversion.

The Answer: Firstly, there can be no jealousy, contention, and conflict in the matters of the hereafter, so if any of those societies attempts to compete or strive against another it will be as though it is hypocritical and dissembling in worship.

Secondly: We congratulate all societies founded out of love of religion and we unite with them, on two conditions:

First Condition: That they preserve the freedom which is in accordance with the Shari'a and public order.

Second Condition: That they act out of love, and do not smear other groups for self-advantage. If any are in error, they should refer it to the religious authorities, who collectively constitute the Mufti of the Umma.

Thirdly: Any society whose aim is upholding the Word of God cannot in any way be the means of animosity and serving its own ends. Even if it wants to, it will not be successful, because to do so is duplicity. The truth is exalted, and may not by sacrificed for anything. Can the Pleiades be swept with a brush or eaten like a bunch of grapes? Anyone who puffs at the sun of reality to extinguish it merely advertises his lunacy.

Newspapers and periodicals which support religion! We say that religious groups and societies should have a common goal. But it is neither possible for them to unite in their ways and methods, nor is it permissible. For it opens up the way blind imitation and causes people to say: "What is it to me? Let others do the thinking."

Eighth Groundless Fear: The majority of the people who have joined the Union here, both in fact and in spirit, supporters of Islamic Unity, are ordinary people, and some are an unknown quantity; this hints of conflict and dissension.

The Answer: It is rather as a consequence of enmity not being permitted. Also, since its aim is unity and upholding the Word of God, all its activities and endeavours are worship. In the mosque of worship king and beggar are equal. True equality is its principle; there is no privilege. The best is the one most fearing of God. And the one most fearing of God is the most humble. As a consequence, together with joining in meaning the true

Union,[6] he will be honoured by joining this Union, which is a physical sample of it. A single droplet does not increase the ocean. And just as one grievous sin does not cause a person to cease being a believer, so the door of repentance is open till the sun rises in the west. And in the same way that a flagon of impure water does not make the ocean unclean, a number of persons of unknown origins —now that they have purified themselves— who have joined this sample of Islamic Unity with the firm intention, as far as they can, to revive the practices of the Prophet (PBUH), obey his commands and refrain from what he prohibited, and not disturb public order, will not stain this elevated reality. For even if they themselves are tainted, their belief is sacred. The bond too is belief. One who smears this sacred name with such pretexts, is unaware of Islam's worth and elevatedness, and simply proclaims himself to be an idiot. We strenuously reject any innuendoes made against our society, which is a sample of Islamic Unity, by analogies made with worldly societies, and efforts to smear it. If anyone offers objections by way of asking for information, we are ready to reply to them. The field is open...!

The society of which I am a member is Islamic Unity, which I have here described in detail. It is not the imaginary organization that critics have falsely described. The members of this religious association are together whether in the north, south, east or west.

Question: You sometimes sign yourself as Bediuzzaman (the Wonder of the Age). Does this not infer self-praise?

The Answer: It is not for praise; I declare my faults, excuses, and apologies with this title. Because 'Bedi''

---

6. That is, Islamic Unity. [Tr.]

means strange. And like my form, my conduct, my manner of address, and my attire are all strange and different. Through the tongue of this manner and title I request that the current reasoning and styles based on customary practice are not made the measure and criterion for my style and reasoning. Also my aims are strange and unusual. I have illustrated the lines:

> *I have become the target of every weird person;*
> *For I am weird in the eyes of the weird!*

An example is this: I have been in Istanbul one year and have seen a hundred years' worth of revolutions.

Peace be on those who follow right-guidance!

We say in the name of all believers: Long live the Shari'a of Muhammad (Upon whom be blessings and peace)!

Bediuzzaman
Said Nursi

* * *

Letter to Dervish Vahdeti

Volkan No: 105
24 Rebîülevvel 1327/ 2 Nisan 1325/ 15 April 1909

My Brother, the Editor!

Writers should be mannerly, and their manners should be moulded by the manners of Islam. Let the sense of religion in the conscience order the Press Regulations, for this Islamic revolution has shown that what governs all consciences is Islamic zeal, the light of lights. Also, it has been understood that Islamic Unity includes all the people of Islam; there is no one outside it.

Said Nursi

* * *

Address to Our Heroic Soldiers

Volkan No: 107
26 Rebîülevvel 1327/ 4 Nisan 1325/ 17 April 1909

[This piece and the next one, parts of an address to the army during the events in April 1909 known as the 31st March Incident, induced eight mutinying regiments to obey their officers and return to barracks, greatly lessening the harm of the calamity.]

Noble soldiers of Islam! Mighty heroes who have twice saved this oppressed nation and sacred Islam from a terrible abyss! Your beauty and perfection lie in order and discipline. You demonstrated this perfectly at the time of greatest confusion. Yes, your life and strength lie in obedience. Display this sacred virtue before even your least officer. The honour of thirty million Ottomans and three hundred million Muslims is tied to your obedience. The banner of Divine Unity is in the hand of your courage, while the strength of those blessed hands of yours is obedience. Your officers are your compassionate fathers. Both the Qur'an, and Hadith, and wisdom and experience state that obedience to those in command who are rightful is obligatory.

You know that thirty million could not bring about two such revolutions in a hundred years. The true strength resulting from your obedience made the whole Islamic nation grateful to you. This honour may be confirmed

now through obedience to your officers. The honour of
Islam is also dependent on that obedience. I know that
you did not get mixed up with it in order to save your
officers —who are like your kind fathers— from responsibility. But the matter is finished now, so you should
throw yourselves into their compassionate embrace. The
Illustrious Shari'a orders you to do this. For your officers
have been charged with authority over you; for the benefit of the country and nation, and particularly to maintain discipline in the army, obedience to those charged
with authority is obligatory. The Shari'a of Muhammad
(Upon whom be blessings and peace) will also be pre-
served through your obedience.

Said Nursi

* * *

Address to the Army

Volkan No: 110
29 Rebîülevvel 1327/ 7 Nisan 1325/ 20 April 1909

O Soldiers of Islam! I remind you of the decree of the Glory of the World (Upon whom be blessings and peace) that it is obligatory to obey those in command within the bounds of the Shari'a. Your commanders and masters are your officers. The army resembles a huge and orderly factory. If one cog of the machinery departs from the order and discipline, the whole factory is thrown into confusion.

Your orderly and powerful factory of the army is the point of support and source of help of thirty million Ottomans and three hundred million Muslims.

Your bloodless and instantaneous killing of two awesome despotisms was wondrous; you exhibited two miracles of the Illustrious Shari'a, offering two proofs to those weak in belief of the power of Islamic zeal and the sacredness of the Shari'a. Had the price of these two revolutions been thousands of martyrs, we still would have considered it cheap. But if even a thousandth of your obedience is sacrificed, it will turn out extremely expensive for us. For any decrease in your obedience is the cause of death, like a drop in the life-force or in body-heat.

History has always testified to the awesome harms to country and nation when soldiers interfere in politics. Certainly your Islamic zeal will prevent you from attempting things that will cause harm to the life of

Islam. Those who will think of politics are your officers and commanders, who are like your powers of thought.

Sometimes, since it repels considerable harm politically, a matter you consider to be harmful is pure benefit; your officers see this due to their experience, and give you commands. It is not then permissible for you to be hesitant. Actions in personal life that are contrary to the Shari'a do not negate skill and expertise in a craft, and do not make the craft abhorrent. The illicit private conduct of a skilful doctor or proficient engineer does not prevent their medicine and engineering being profited from. So do not fail in your obedience because of minor actions contrary to the Shari'a of some of your officers who are experienced in the science of warfare, skilful in that art, and whose ideas are enlightened through their Islamic zeal. Because the science of warfare is an important art. Also, since your rebellion showed the Illustrious Shari'a like the Shining Hand of Moses, you compelled those few unlawful actions to return to the fold of the Shari'a. This licit union of yours swallowed up other societies which were the cause of division and confusion of ideas, like the Staff of Moses. It also compelled the magicians to prostrate. Your action in this revolution was like a medicine, but if excessive, it will turn into poison and head the life of Islam towards a serious illness. Also, through your endeavours the despotism with us has for the present been destroyed. But we are still oppressed by Europe in respect of progress. The utmost caution and moderation are needed.

Long live the Illustrious Shari'a! Long live the army!

Said Nursi

* * *

A Important Warning
to the Societies and Clubs

Our society is now a constitutional government. The harm of having governments within the government has become apparent. The fact that there is not a uniform level of culture has resulted in enmity, bigotry, and partisanship between the parties. It has become a field favourable to those nurturing hatred, who by exploiting that natural force, meddle in politics and exercise arbitrary power —which is pleasurable— in the general administration. It is therefore extremely harmful for the groups and parties to continue in their present form, although it may be beneficial for members of a company, or intellectuals or unbiased people to criticize politics, or for people of learning to offer advice and counsel to one another. Our constitutional government now forms the society.

Bediuzzaman
Said Nursi

* * *

Second Addendum
First Part

Seeds of Reality

[This consists of aphorisms taken from a collection published thirty-five years ago called Seeds of Reality]

In the Name of God, the Merciful,
the Compassionate.

All praise be to God, the Sustainer of All the Worlds,
and blessings and peace be upon our master Muhammad,
and on all his Family and Companions.

1. The prescription for a sick age, an ailing nation, an ill member, is to follow the Qur'an.

2. The prescription for a glorious though unfortunate continent, an illustrious though hapless state, a noble though ownerless people, is Islamic Unity.

3. One who does not have the strength to raise and turn the earth and all the stars and suns as though they

were beads of a *tesbih* cannot lay claim to creating anything in the universe. For everything is tied to everything else.

4. The raising to life of all animate beings at the resurrection of the dead can be no more difficult for Divine Power than restoring to life a fly in the spring, heavy with the death-stained sleep of winter. For Pre-Eternal Power is essential; it does not change; impotence cannot penetrate it; obstacles cannot intervene in it; there can be no degrees in it; everything is the same in relation to it.

5. He who created the eye of the mosquito is the one who created the sun.

6. The one who ordered the stomach of a flea is also the one who ordered the solar system.

7. There is such miraculousness in the universe's compilation that if to suppose the impossible all natural causes possessed will and the power to act, they would still prostrate in utter impotence before such miraculousness, exclaiming: "Glory be unto You! We have no power; indeed You are the Mighty, the Wise!"

8. An actual effect has not been given to causes, for Divine Unity and Glory require it to be thus. Only, in the outer aspect of things, causes are a veil to the Hand of Power; and this, Divine Dignity and Grandeur require, so that in the superficial view the Hand of Power should not be seen to be directly in contact with lowly things.

9. The inner dimensions of things, where Divine Power has its connection, are transparent and pure.

10. The Manifest World is a lace veil strewn over the Worlds of the Unseen.

11. An infinite power sufficient to create all the universe is necessary to create a single point and set it in its place. For every letter of this Mighty Book of the Universe, and particularly all its living letters, has a face looking to all the sentences, and an eye that beholds them.

12. It is well-known: they all looked for the crescent moon of the 'Id, but no one could see it. An elderly man swore he had seen it. But what he had seen was not the crescent moon; it was a curved white eyelash. What is an eyelash compared with the moon?... What is the motion of minute particles compared with the one who fashions all beings?

13. Nature resembles a printing-press, not the printer. It is an embroidery, not the Embroiderer. It is passive, not active. It is a pattern, not a source. It is an order, and not the Orderer. It is a law, not a Power. It is a code of laws proceeding from a will, not an external reality.

14. The lure and attraction in the conscience, which is the essential nature of conscious beings, is felt through the appeal of a drawing truth.

15. The essential nature of beings does not lie. The inclination to grow in a seed declares: "I shall sprout and produce fruit!" It speaks the truth. In an egg is the desire for life; it says: "I shall be a hen!," and this comes about, with Divine permission. It speaks the truth. Due to the inclination to freeze, a handful of water says: "I shall take up more space!," and unyielding iron cannot give it the lie; the rightness of its words splits the iron. These inclinations are the manifestations of the creative commands proceeding from Divine Will.

16. Pre-Eternal Power, which does not leave ants without

a prince, or bees without a queen, certainly does not leave mankind without prophets. As the Splitting of the Moon was a miracle of Muhammad (PBUH) for men in the Manifest World, so the Ascension was a supreme miracle of His before the angels and spirit beings in the World of the Inner Dimensions of Things. Through this clear wonder, the sainthood of his prophethood was proved, and like lightening or the moon, that shining Being scattered light through those inner worlds.

17. The two phrases of the confession of faith testify to each other. The first is 'the proof of cause to effect' of the second, while the second is 'the proof of effect to cause' of the first.

18. Life is a sort of manifestation of Unity within multiplicity, and therefore leads to unity. Life makes one thing the owner of everything.

19. Spirit is a law possessing external existence, a conscious law. Like the stable and enduring laws of creation, spirit comes from the World of the Divine Command and the attribute of Will. Divine Power clothes it an existence decked out with senses. He makes a subtle, flowing being the shell to that jewel. Existent spirit is the brother of the conceivable law. They are both enduring and come from the World of the Divine Command. If Pre-Eternal Power had clothed the laws governing in the species of beings in external existence, they would have been spirits. And if the spirit banishes consciousness, it still would be an undying law.

20. Beings are visible through light, and their existence is known through life. Both are revealers.

21. Christianity will either erupt, or being purified, will

lay down its arms before Islam. Christianity was split apart several times, and Protestantism emerged. Then Protestantism was rent, and approached the true affirmation of Divine Unity. It is preparing to be rent again. It will either erupt and be extinguished, or it will see before it the truths of Islam, which encompass the basis of true Christianity, and it will lay down its arms.

The Prophet Muhammad (Upon whom be blessings and peace) alluded to this great mystery when he said: "Jesus will appear having descended from the skies; he will be of my community and will act in accordance with my Shari'a."

22. It is the sacredness of the authority more than proof that drives the mass of the people to conform.

23. The essentials and incontestable matters of religion, which form ninety-nine per cent, are each diamond pillars, while the controversial matters which are open to interpretation form only ten per cent. Ninety diamond pillars may not be put under the protection of ten gold pillars. Books and interpretations should be telescopes for observing the Qur'an; they should be mirrors; not shadows or deputies!

24. Anyone who is capable may make interpretations of the Law for his own self; but he cannot make the Law.

25. Calling others to accept an idea is dependent on acceptance by the 'Ulama; otherwise it is innovation, and should be rejected.

26. Since by nature man is noble, he seeks the truth. Sometimes he encounters the false, but supposing it to be the truth preserves it in his heart. Then, when delving into reality, without his willing it, mis-

guidance strikes him on the head; supposing it to be reality, he plunges his head into it.

27. Divine Power has many mirrors, each more subtle and transparent than the last; they vary from water to air, and air to ether, and ether to the World of Similitudes; from the World of Similitudes to the World of Spirits, and even to time, and to thought. A single word in the mirror of the air becomes millions of words. The Pen of Power writes this mystery of reproduction in truly wondrous manner. The reflection contains either its identity or its identity together with its nature. The images of dense beings are moving but dead. While the images of a luminous spirit in their own mirrors are living and linked with it; even if they are not identical, they are not other than it.

28. Since the sun shakes itself in its axial rotation, its fruits do not fall; whereas if it did not shake itself, the planets would fall and be scattered.

29. If the light of thought is not illuminated with the light of the heart and blended with it, it is darkness and breeds tyranny. If the white of the eye, which resembles day, was not together with its black pupil, which resembles night, the eye would not be the eye; it would be unseeing. Similarly, if the black core of the heart is not present in white thought, it lacks insight.

30. If knowledge lacks the insight of the heart, it is ignorance. Taking the part of something is one thing, belief is something else.

31. Embroidering meaningless things is to mislead simple minds.

32. A learned guide should be a sheep, not a bird. A sheep gives its lamb milk, while a bird gives its chick regurgitated food.

33. The existence of something is dependent on the existence of all its parts. As for non-existence, since it occurs though non-existence of one part, a weak man supports destruction in order to demonstrate his power; he acts negatively instead of positively.

34. If the laws of government are not combined with the principles of wisdom, and the bonds of force not combined with the laws of truth, they will not be fruitful among the mass of the people.

35. Tyranny has donned the hat of justice; treachery has clothed itself in the garment of patriotism; *jihad* has been given the name of rebellion; captivity has been called freedom! Opposites have exchanged forms!

36. Politics which revolves around benefit is savagery.

37. To show friendliness towards a hungry beast does not excite its compassion, but its hunger. Both its fangs and its claws will want their rent!

38. Time has shown that Paradise is not cheap, and neither is Hell unnecessary.

39. While the virtues of those known by the world as the upper classes should be the cause of modesty and humility, they have lead to oppression and arrogance. And while the poverty and powerlessness of the poor and common people should be the cause of compassion and bounty, they have resulted in captivity and condemnation.

40. So long as honour and good things are to be obtained from a thing, they offer it to the upper classes, but if it is a bad thing, they divide it among the ordinary people.

41. If there is no imagined goal, or if it is forgotten or pretended to be forgotten, thoughts perpetually revolve around the 'I'.

42. The origin of all revolutions and corruption, and the spur and source of all base morals are just two sayings:

   The First Saying: "So long as I'm full, what is it to me if others die of hunger?"

   The Second Saying: "You suffer hardship so that I can live in ease; you work so that I can eat."

   There is only one remedy for extirpating the First Saying, and that is the obligatory payment of *zakat*. While the remedy for the Second is the prohibition of usury and interest. Qur'anic justice stands at the door of the world and says to usury and interest: "No entry! It is forbidden! You don't have the right to enter here!" Mankind did not heed the command, and received a severe blow. So it must heed it before it receives one even more severe!

43. War between nations and states is relinquishing its place to war between the classes of mankind. For just as man does not want to be a slave, so he does not want to be a labourer.

44. Someone who follows his goal by an illicit path is usually punished by receiving the opposite of what he intended. The recompense for illicit love, like love for Europe, is the cruel enmity of the beloved.

45. The past and calamities should be considered with regard to Divine Determining, while the future and sins from the point of view of responsibility before God. The Jabariyya and Mu'tazila are reconciled on this point.

46. Impotence should not be resorted to in things for which a solution may be found, while for things for which there is no solution, punishment should not be resorted to.

47. The wounds of life may be healed. But Islamic pride and honour, and national pride, their wounds are extremely deep.

48. It sometimes happens that a single word causes an army to perish, and one bullet leads to the annihilation of thirty million.[1] Some conditions are such that a small act raises man to the highest of the high, while others are such that a small action reduces him to the lowest of the low.

49. One grain of truth consumes a stack of lies. One grain of reality is superior to a stack of illusions. Everything you say should be true, but it is not right to say everything true.

50. A person who sees the good in things has good thoughts. And he who has good thoughts receives pleasure from life.

51. What gives life to people is hope, while what kills them is despair.

52. Since early days, this Islamic state took on itself the upholding of the Word of God, the maintenance of independence, and *jihad* for Islam, an obligation which if undertaken by part of the community, released the rest; it considered itself to be charged with sacrificing itself for Islam, which was united, and carrying the banner of the Caliphate. The misfortune it now suffers will therefore be made up for by the future prosperity and freedom of the Islamic World. For this calamity has speeded up in wondrous fashion the growth of Islamic brotherhood, the leaven of our lives.

---

1. A single bullet fired by a Serbian soldier at the Austrian Crown-Prince set off the Great War, and was the cause of thirty million souls being lost.

53. To attribute to Christianity the virtues of civilization, which are not its property, and to show retrogression, the enemy of Islam, to be its friend, is to suggest that the firmament is revolving in the opposite direction.

54. A tarnished, matchless diamond is always superior to a piece of glistening glass.

55. Those who seek everything in materiality know only what their eyes see, and such eyes are blind in spiritual matters.

56. If metaphors fall from the hands of learning into those of ignorance, they are transformed into their literal meanings, opening the door to superstition.

57. Favour greater than Divine favour is not favour. Everything has to be described as it is.

58. Fame also ascribes to man what is not his.

59. Hadiths are the source of life and inspirer of reality.

60. The revival of religion is the revival of the nation. The life of religion is the light of life.

61. The Qur'an, which is a mercy for mankind, only accepts a civilization that comprises the happiness of all, or at least of the majority. Modern civilization has been founded on five negative principles:

   1. Its point of support is force, the mark of which is aggression.

   2. Its aim and goal is benefit, the mark of which is jostling and tussling.

   3. Its principle in life is conflict, the mark of which is strife.

   4. The bond between the masses is racialism and negative nationalism, which is nourished through devouring others; its mark is collision.

5. Its enticing service is inciting lust and passion and gratifying the desires. But lust transforms man into a beast.

However, the civilization the Shari'a of Muhammad (PBUH) comprises and commands is this: its point of support is truth instead of force, the mark of which is justice and harmony. Its goal is virtue in place of benefit, the mark of which is love and attraction. Its means of unity are the ties of religion, country, and class, in place of racialism and nationalism, and the mark of these is sincere brotherhood, peace, and only defence against external aggression. In life is the principle of mutual assistance instead of the principle of conflict, the mark of which is accord and solidarity. And it offers guidance instead of lust, the mark of which is human progress and spiritual advancement.

Do not loosen your hands from Islam, the preserver of our existence; cling onto it with all your strength, or you shall be lost!

62. A general disaster results from the error of the majority. Disaster is the result of crime, and the introduction to reward.

63. A martyr thinks he is alive. Since he did not suffer the pangs of death, he considers the life he sacrificed to be perpetual and not to have been severed. Only, he finds it purer.

64. The pure justice of the Qur'an does not spill the life and blood of an innocent, even for the whole of humanity. The two are the same both in the view of Divine Power, and in the view of justice. But through self-interest man becomes such that he will destroy everything that forms an obstacle to his ambition,

even the world if he can, and he will wipe out man-kind.

65. Fear and weakness encourage outside influences.

66. Definite benefits should not be sacrificed for imaginary harms.

67. Istanbul politics at the present time are a sickness like Spanish 'flu.

68. Tell a bad man, "You are good, you are good," and it is not unheard of that he will become good. And tell a good man "You are bad, you are bad," and it is not rare for him to become bad.

69. So long as the enemy of an enemy remains his enemy, he is a friend; while so long as the friend of an enemy remains his friend, he is an enemy.

70. Obduracy is this: if Satan assists someone, he calls him "an angel," and calls down blessings on him. But if among his opponents he encounters an angel, he calls him "a satan who has changed his clothes," and curses him.

71. The remedy for one ill person may be poison for another. If a remedy exceeds its limit, it is the cause of ills.

72. Solidarity in a society results in tranquility in all its activites, while mutual envy causes all its activities to come to a standstill.

73. If the community is not one and a whole, undivided number, addition makes smaller, like multiplying fractions.[2]

---

2. It is well-known that in arithmetic, multiplication and addition increase: four times four makes sixteen. While fractions, contrary to multiplication and addition, make smaller: a third multiplied by a third makes a ninth. In just the same way, if there is not integral wholeness, correctness, and unity among people, by multiplying they become smaller, spoilt, and without value.

74. Non-acceptance is confused with the acceptance of non-being. The evidence for non-acceptance is the absence of established proof. The acceptance of non-being requires proof of non-being. One is doubt while the other is denial.

75. If doubt in the matters of belief destroys one, or even a hundred, evidences, it does not harm what is posited; for there are hundreds of evidences.

76. The majority of Muslims should be followed. For when they followed the majority, the Umayyads, who were slack in religion, finally entered the Sunni community. As for the Shi'a, who were firm in religion but remained in the minority as regards their practices, finally only a part of them followed the Rafida.

77. If unanimity concerning good leads to conflict concerning what is better, then sometimes good is better than the better; right is truer than what is truer. Everyone should say about his own way that "It is right," he should not say "it is the only right way." Or he should say, "it is good," but he should not say "it is the only good way."

78. If there was no Paradise, Hell would not be torment.

79. As time grows older, the Qur'an grows younger; it signs become apparent. Like light sometimes appears as fire, sometimes intense eloquence appears as exaggeration.

80. Degrees in heat occur through the intervention of cold; the degrees of beauty occur through the intervention of ugliness. Pre-Eternal Power is essential, necessary, and inherent. Impotence cannot penetrate it; there can be no degrees it in; everything is equal in relation to it.

81. The sun's image, which is the effulgence of its man-
    ifestation, displays the same identity on the surface of
    the sea and in all its droplets.

82. Life is a manifestation of Unity; Unity is also its con-
    sequence.

83. So long as it remains unknown who are the saints
    among men, which moment prayers are accepted on
    Fridays, which night in Ramadan is the Night of
    Power, and which among the Divine Names is the
    Greatest Name, other things retain their value and
    importance is given to them. Twenty years of doubt-
    ful life is preferable to a thousand years' life the end
    of which is specified.

84. The consequence of sin in this world is evidence for
    its punishment in the hereafter.

85. In the view of Power, sustenance is as important as
    life. Power brings into existence, Divine Determining
    clothes in form, Divine favour nurtures. Life is a
    summary, a specified product and is apparent. Sus-
    tenance is not a summary; it is gradual and wide-
    spread, and causes thought. There is no death from
    hunger, for death occurs before the food stored up in
    the body in the form of fat is exhausted. That is to say,
    illness resulting from the giving up of habit kills, not
    lack of sustenance.

86. The licit sustenance of carniverous wild animals are
    the innumerable remains of dead animals; they both
    cleanse the face of the earth, and they find their food.

87. Before entering the mouth and disappearing down the
    throat, a mouthful worth one *kurush* and one worth
    ten are the same. There is only a few seconds' differ-
    ence in the mouth. To raise the price from one to ten
    in order to gratify and please the sense of taste, which

is like an inspector and doorkeeper, is most prodigal and wasteful.

88. When pleasure calls, a person should say: "It is as though I ate it." (*Sanki yedim.*) For one who made that his principle, could have eaten a mosque called "*Sanki Yedim,*" but he did not.[3]

89. Formerly, there was no hunger among Muslims; there was the desire for ease. Now they are hungry, and they have no wish for pleasure.

90. Temporary pains should be smiled on rather than temporary pleasure being smiled on, and should be welcomed. For past pleasures cause one to say: "Alas!", and "Alas!" is the interpreter of a concealed pain. While past pains cause one to say: "Oh!", and "Oh!" tells of a permanent pleasure and bounty.

91. Forgetfulness is also a bounty. It allows one to suffer the pains of only one day, and causes the rest to be forgotten.

92. In every calamity is a degree of bounty, like a degree of heat. Greater calamities should be thought of and the degree of bounty in the small one noted, and God should be thanked. For if the calamity is blown up, it will grow; and if it is worried over, it will double; the image, the imagining, in the heart will be transformed into reality; and that will pound the heart as well.

93. In society as a whole, everyone has a window, known as rank, through which to see and be seen. If the window is higher than his stature, a person will grow taller through arrogance; and if it is lower than his stature, he will bow down through modesty so to see

---

3. That is, the person put aside the money saved through his abstinence and built the mosque with the proceeds. It is in the Fatih district of Istanbul. [Tr.]

and be seen at that level. The measure of greatness in man is smallness, that is, modesty. The scale of smallness is bigness; that is, arrogance.

94. The dignity of the weak before the strong becomes arrogance in the strong; while the modesty of the strong before the weak becomes abasement in the weak. The seriousness of someone in authority in their office is dignity, and his humility is abasement. While his seriousness in his house is haughtiness, and his humility, modesty. If an individual is on his own, then his tolerance and self-sacrifice are good acts. But if he is more than one, they are treachery and inauspicious. Someone should swallow his pride in his own name and not be boastful, but he may boast in the name of the nation and should not swallow his pride.

95. To 'leave it to others' in planning the preliminaries of a matter is laziness, while in awaiting the outcome it is reliance on God. Resignation with the fruits of one's labour and with fate is contentment, and strengthens the wish to strive. Whereas making do with what exists is to lack enterprise.

96. Just as there is obedience and rebellion in the face of the commands of the Shari'a, so too there is obedience and rebellion in the face of the creative commands in the universe. With regard to the first, the reward and punishment are mostly in the hereafter, while with the second, they are mostly in this world. For example, the reward of patience is victory; the punishment for idleness is poverty; the reward of effort is wealth, and the reward of constancy, triumph. Justice without equality is not justice.

97. Mutual resemblance is the cause of contradiction; congruity is the basis of solidarity; smallness of

character is the source of arrogance; weakness is the source of pride; impotence is the source of opposition; and curiosity is the teacher of knowledge.

98. Through need, and especially through hunger, the Creator's Power has reined in foremost man, and all the animals, and put them in order. Also, He saved the world from anarchy, and making need the master of civilization, ensured progress.

99. Distress teaches vice. Despair is the source of misguidance; and darkness of heart, the source of distress of the spirit.

100. When due to infatuation, men become amiable, women become masculine by being impudent.

A beautiful woman entering a gathering of brothers awakens hypocrisy, rivalry, and envy. That is to say, the unveiling of women led to the unveiling of bad morals in civilized man.

101. The represented forms of little smiling corpses have played a large role in making the evil-polluted perverse spirit of modern man what it is.

102. The prohibited statue is either petrified tyranny, or embodied lust, or personified hypocrisy.

103. For someone who has truly entered into the bounds of Islam by conforming precisely to its incontestable matters, the desire to expand is the desire to be perfected. But for someone who may be counted outside those bounds through slackness, the desire to expand is the desire to destroy. In time of storm and earthquake, it is advisable to not open the door of *ijtihad*, and to close the windows too. The overly free and easy should not be indulged with dispensations, but determinedly and severely warned.

104. Unfortunate truths become worthless in worthless hands.

105. Our globe resembles a living being; it displays the signs of life. If it was to be reduced to the size of an egg, would it not become a sort of animal? Or if a microbe was enlarged to the size of the globe, would it not resemble it? If it has life, it has a spirit too. If the world was reduced to the size of man, and the stars made like the particles and substance of his being, would that not also be a living conscious being? God has many such animals.

106. There are two Shari'as:

The First is the Shari'a that we know which orders the actions and conduct of man, the microcosm, and proceeds from the attribute of Speech.

The Second is the Supreme Shari'a of Creation, which orders the motion and rest of the world, the macroanthropos, proceeds from the attribute of Will, and is sometimes wrongly called Nature. The angels are a vast community; they are the bearers, representatives, and personifications of the creative commands which proceed from the attribute of Will and are the Shari'a of Creation.

107. If you weigh the senses of a microscopic organism against man's senses, you will observe a strange mystery: man is in the form of *Ya. Sin.*, inscribed in him is the *Sura Ya. Sin.*

108. Materialism is a spiritual plague which has infected man with a fearsome fever, causing him to be visited by Divine wrath. The more the ability to inculcate and criticize expands, so does that plague spread.

109. The most wretched, distressed, and suffering of men is the man with no work. For idleness is the cousin of non-existence, while striving is the life of existence and the waking state of life.

110. Profiting from banks, the doors of usury and interest, is for the infidels, who are the worst of mankind, and for the most tyrannous of the former, and for the most base of the latter. They are the cause of absolute harm for the World of Islam, so mankind's affluence should not be taken into consideration. For if the infidels are warmongers and aggressive, so too they are without respect and honour.

111. The *Khutba* in the Friday Prayers is for mentioning the essentials and incontestable matters of religion, not for instructing in theoretical matters. The Arabic terms recall these in more elevated fashion. If Hadiths and Qur'anic verses are balanced, it will be apparent that even the most eloquent of men cannot attain to the verses' eloquence, and cannot resemble them.

Said Nursi

*   *   *

Second Addendum
to the Damascus Sermon

Second Part

An Allusion of Sura al-Ikhlas[1]

*In the Name of God, the Merciful,
the Compassionate.*
*All praise be to God, the Sustainer of All the Worlds,
and peace and blessings be upon Muhammad,
the Chief of His Messengers.*

T he specification of *Say, He is* is an allusion to
unity of witnessing: In the view of reality, there
is nothing observed except Him.

God, The One is an explicit statement of Divine Unity:
There is no true object of worship save Him.

God, the Eternally Besought One alludes to the unity
of Divine dominicality: There is no Creator and Sustainer
save Him. It is also a sign to the unity of Divine might

---

1. Qur'an, Sura 112.

and power: There is no Self-Subsistent and no absolutely Self-Sufficient One save Him.

He begets not alludes to the unity of Divine Glory, and rejects every sort of association of partners with God. That is, one who is subject to change or division, or who reproduces, cannot be God. It rejects association of partners with God in the form of 'the ten intellects,' or the angels, Jesus or Uzayr being Divine offspring.

And neither is He begotten proves the pre-eternity of God and His Unity. It rejects ascribing partners to God in the form of causality, the worship of stars, idolatry, and Naturalism. That is, something created or detached from its original, or born of some matter cannot be God.

And there is none like unto Him is a comprehensive affirmation of Divine Unity. That is, He has no like, partner, or peer either in His essence, or in His attributes, or in His actions. *There is nothing whatever like unto Him, and He is All-Hearing, All-Seeing.*[2]

This Sura of the Qur'an rejects all forms of associating partners with God, and its six phrases comprise seven degrees of the affirmation of Divine Unity. Each phrase is both the result and the proof of the others.

Together with all its parts and members, and even its cells and all its particles, the universe, which is the supreme affirmer of Divine Unity and its greatest proof, declares "There is no god save God," like a Mevlevi dervish mentioning God's Names, all contributing to the resounding sound of this mighty proof, as tongues affirming Divine Unity.

If you fasten your ear to the breast of the Qur'an, which is the articulate proof of Divine Unity, you will

---

2. Qur'an, 42:11.

hear from the depths of its heart an utterly elevated, serious, heartfelt, familiar, convincing, heavenly voice, decked out with proofs, which continually chants: "There is no god but God."

The six aspects of this illumined proof are all transparent. Above it is the stamp of miraculousness; within it are the lights of guidance; beneath it are proof and logic; on its right is its calling the intellect to investigate; on its left is its calling the conscience to testify; before it is good; its goal is the happiness of both worlds; and its point of support is pure revelation. How can doubts and delusions penetrate it?

* * *

Will, mind, emotion, and the subtle inner faculties, which constitute the four elements of the conscience and four faculties of the spirit, each have an ultimate aim. The ultimate aim of the will is worship of God; that of the mind is knowledge of God; that of the emotions is love of God; and that of the inner faculties is the vision of God. The perfect worship known as taqwa comprises the four. The Shari'a both cultivates these, and corrects them, and takes them towards their ultimate goals.

* * *

If the means and causes in creation had been given an actual effect, they should also have been given universal consciousness, and this would have been opposed to the perfect art in things. However, the excellence of the art in things, from the lowest to the highest and from the smallest to the greatest, is proportionate to the innate stature of each. Thus, some are not close to the True Causer and some far from Him, and some of them are not created through intermediaries and some without. The lack of perfection in man's voluntary works rejects the ideas of compulsion and proves will.

It is worthy of notice that in respect of order, a city built by men as the work of their intellects through the intervention of their wills is inferior to the bee community in their hive, which is the fruit of inspiration. While the city of cells of the honeycomb, the bees' exhibition of art, is inferior as regards order to the fruit of the pomegranate and its flower. This means that from whichever pen the general attraction in the universe flows, the miniscule attraction in the most minute indivisible particles are that pen's points.

Islam says: *There is no god but God*, and does not accept that causes and intermediaries have an actual effect. It looks on intermediaries as signifying the meaning of one other than themselves. Belief in Divine Unity and the duties of submission to it demand this. However, because it has been corrupted, present-day Christianity considers causes and intermediaries to have an effect, and looks on them as signifying themselves. Their belief in Jesus as the son of God and in the priesthood demands this, and urges it. They look on their saints for their own sakes as though they do not signify another, as the source of effulgence, like the light of a lamp —according to one view— transformed from the sunlight. We look on the saints as signifying the meaning of another, that is, as a place of reflection and manifestation, like a mirror spreads the sunlight.[3]

---

3. The Naqshbandis' method is based on this mystery.

It is because of this that spiritual journeying begins from humility, passes through self-abasement, and reaches the station of annihilation in God. It begins to journey through infinite stations. Such journeying is extinguished by the arrogant pride of the ego and evil-commanding soul. However, not true Christianity, but the corrupted Christianity which has been shaken by philosophy, strengthens the ego. If a person of high rank and station with a powerful ego is a Christian, he becomes more determined in his religion, whereas a Muslim in a similar position becomes lax in religion.

* * *

The intense and varying pleasure in activity as it passes from the potential to the actual is the leaven of change in the universe and the nucleus of the law through which all things are perfected. Stepping out of prison into a garden, and passing from a seed to a shoot is the same pleasure. If activity incorporates change, the pleasure increases immeasurably. It is this that causes the hardship in duties to be borne. However attractive for intelligent creatures is absolute perfection, for unintelligent creatures activity is attractive to the same degree and encourages effort. It is for this reason that ease is hardship and hardship, ease.

* * *

• Greed and precipitancy are the cause of loss. For the greedy and hasty person will not act in accordance with the successive causes in creation, like the steps of a staircase, and therefore will not be successful. Even if he is, since he skips some of the steps of the natural progression, he falls into despair, and then, when overcome by heedlessness, the door is opened to him.

• God Almighty created the inner heart for belief and for knowledge and love of Himself, while the outer heart He designed for other things. Criminal greed pierces the heart, and introduces idols into it. God is displeased and punishes the greedy person with the opposite of his purpose.

• The scoundrels who because of ambition took political thought to the places of Islamic beliefs did not receive honour and glory, but were execrated and reviled. The frustration and despair of sensual love arise from this same greed and ambition. All the poetry about this sort of love are the lamentations of mourning.

• If you anxiously try to sleep at night, you will chase sleep away and remain awake.

• There are two beggars, one persistently importunate, the other reserved and self-contained. A further example of this extensive law is that one would rather give to the latter.

* * *

Our worst calamity and sickness is that criticism which is based on pride and deception. If fairness utilizes criticism, it pares the truth. Whereas if it is pride that employs it, it mutilates and destroys it. The very worst sort is that which is levelled at the tenets of belief and questions of religion. For belief comprises both affirmation, and exercise of the mind, and commitment, and surrender, and compliance. Criticism of this sort destroys the compliance, commitment, and mental exercise. Rather than affirming, the person feels uncommitted. At this time of doubts and hesitation, it is necessary to look favourably on the positive ideas and encouraging statements that emerge from luminous, warm hearts, and to foster and strengthen the exercise of the mind and commitment. What they call "unbiased, objective reasoning" is temporary unbelief. Novices and those new to the truth do it.

* * *

The view of the one who taught the Miraculous Qur'an —that Warner and Bringer of Good News— and his critical insight, were too accurate, sublime, clear, and penetrating to confuse and obscure reality with his imagination; and his way of truth is too scupulous, self-sufficient, and elevated to deceive and cheat people.

For the perceptive eye is not deceived, and a truth-seeking heart will not deceive.

* * *

The Qur'an describes the loathsomeness of backbiting with the verse:

> *Would any among you like to eat the flesh of your dead brother?*[4]

With six phrases, on six levels, it severely censures the backbiter. It is as follows:

---

4. Qur'an, 49:12.

With its interrogative form it says: "Think! Could such a thing be permitted? If your mind is not sound, look at your heart; could it love such a thing? And if your heart is not sound, examine your conscience; would it consent to destroying the life of society, as though tearing off your own flesh with your own teeth? And if you have no social conscience, examine your humanity; could it have such an appetite and such monstrous rapacity? If you have no humanity, think of fellow-feeling; could it incline towards an action that would break its own back? And if you have no humanity, is your inborn nature so completely corrupted that you tear at a corpse with your bare teeth?

That is to say, backbiting is repugnant to man's mind, heart, conscience, humanity, fellow-feeling, and inborn nature, as well as to the Shari'a, and is therefore to be utterly rejected.

* * *

The person who does not understand the true meaning of co-operation is more lifeless than a stone. For some stones arch themselves to co-operate with their brothers. Such a stone, despite being a stone, leans towards his brother in the dome when he leaves the builder's hand and bows his head so it touches his brother's head, and so they keep from falling.

That is, the stones of domes stand shoulder to shoulder so as not to fall.

* * *

The unique being at the centre of the conical successive chain from the smallest indivisible particle to man and from man to the sun of suns, is man the ennobled.

* * *

Man possesses senses other than the well-known ones; he has an impelling sense like the sense of taste, and a sense of longing. He possesses too numerous unconscious senses.

* * *

Sometimes desire takes the form of thought, and the greedy person supposes an animal desire to be thought.

* * *

It is strange but some people fall into stinking mud, then to deceive themselves say it is musk and ambergris, and smear it over their faces.

* * *

The martyr is a saint. While being an obligation that if a number of the community undertake it, the rest are absolved, *jihad* has become incumbent on everyone. Indeed, it is now doubly incumbent. As in the Hajj and *zakat*, intention plays little part in *jihad*. However, in point of reality, the lack of intention still resembles intention. That is, if the reverse of the intention is not definitely clear, *jihad* results in true martyrdom. This is because the more the necessity of the *jihad* increases, the more definite it becomes, and the effect of intention, which comprises will, diminishes. If tens of thousands of saints suddenly appear for this sinful nation, it will not be a small reward.

* * *

With us, if someone has strayed from the right path, he is generally immoral and without conscience. For the desire to sin grows by silencing the voice of belief in the conscience. This means that without shaking his conscience and spiritual life, and without holding them in contempt, he cannot commit a completely voluntary evil act. It is for this reason that Islam considers the depraved to be disloyal and traitorous, and does not accept their testimony. It considers apostates to be poison, and sentences them to death. While it recognizes Christian subjects and infidel signatories of a treaty. The Hanafi School accepts the testimony of a non-Muslim subject.

Justice should be executed in the name of religion so that it may be effective over the mind, heart, and spirit, and they may conform to it. Otherwise it affects only the imagination. A criminal is then frightened only of the penalty set by the state, if it is enacted, or he shrinks from the reproaches of the public; if they occur.

* * *

A boat carrying numerous innocent people may not be sunk on account of one criminal. Similarly, enmity should not be nurtured towards a believer who possesses numerous innocent attributes, because of a single criminal attribute.

In particular, belief and the affirmation of Divine Unity, the causes of love, are like Mount Uhud, while the causes of enmity are like pebbles. However unreasonable it is to think of pebbles being heavier than Mount Uhud, for a believer to be hostile towards another believer is lacking in heart to the same degree. Hostility between believers may only take the form of pity.

In Short: Belief demands love, and Islam demands brotherhood.

Words are like goods, wastefulness in them is not permissible.

Said Nursi

* * *

A Letter:

The Qur'anic principles to save awakened mankind

In His Name, be He glorified!

Peace be upon you, and God's mercy and blessings, for ever.

My Dear, True Brothers!

Firstly: I congratulate you with all my heart on all the festivals and holy nights, both those of the past and future, and the material ones and the spiritual ones, and entreat Divine mercy that your prayers and worship are acceptable, and say "Amen" to them.

Secondly: I am compelled to answer privately two of your questions which in many ways are important, and you have frequently asked in meaning:

Your First Question: Why was it that in the early Second Constitutional Period you were passionately involved in politics, yet for nearly forty years now you have given it up completely?

The Answer: I understood with complete certainty that

the ghastly crimes committed by mankind up to the
present sprang from the abuse of the law which is basic
to politics and may be expressed as "Individuals may be
sacrificed for the good of the nation and for the well-
being of the community." Since there is no specified limit
to this fundamental law created by man, it has opened up
the way to excessive abuse. This tyrannical law issued
the *fatwa* for the two World Wars and overturned a thousand years of human progress. So too it permitted the
annihilation of ninety innocents on account of ten crim-
inals. On the pretext of the general good, personal hatred
razed a town because of a single criminal. Since the
Risale-i Nur has proved this fact in some of its collec-
tions and defence speeches, I refer you to them.

Thus, in the face of this tyrannical law of man's politics and diplomacy I discovered the below-mentioned
fundamental laws of the Qur'an of Miraculous Exposition, which comes from the Sublime Throne. They are
expressed by these verses:

> *No bearer of burdens can bear the burdens of
> another.*[1] * *If anyone slays a human being —unless
> it be [in punishment] for murder or for spreading
> corruption on earth— it shall be as though he had
> slain all mankind.*[2]

These two verses teach the following principle: Others are
not answerable for a person's crime. And, without his
consent, an innocent person may not be sacrificed, even
for the whole of mankind. If he voluntarily gives his consent and sacrifices himself, his self-sacrifice is a sort of
martyrdom and is another matter. This establishes true
justice for man. For details I refer you to the Risale-i Nur.

---

1. Qur'an, 6:164, etc.
2. Qur'an, 5:32.

S e c o n d   Q u e s t i o n : While travelling among the nomadic tribes of the east long ago, you used to strongly urge them towards progress and modern civilization. But for nearly forty years now you have called it 'low' civilization, and you have withdrawn from the life of society and gone into seclusion. Why is this?

The Answer: Since modern Western civilization acts contrarily to the fundamental laws of the revealed religions, its evils have come to outweigh its good aspects, and its errors and harmful aspects its benefits; and general tranquillity and a happy worldly life, the true aims of civilization, have been destroyed. And since wastefulness and extravagance have taken the place of frugality and contentment, and laziness and the desire for ease have overcome endeavour and the sense of service, it has made unfortunate mankind both extremely poor and extremely lazy. In explaining the fundamental law of the revealed Qur'an:

Eat and drink, but waste not in excess,[3]

and,

Man possesses naught save that which he strives,[4]

the Risale-i Nur says: "Man's happiness in this life lies in frugality and endeavour, and it is through them that the rich and poor will be reconciled." I shall here make one or two brief points in accordance with this explanation.

The First: In the nomadic stage, man needed only three or four things, and it was only two out of ten who could not obtain them. But now, through wastefulness, abuses, stimulating the appetites, and such things as custom and addiction, present-day civilization has made

---

3. Qur'an, 7:31.
4. Qur'an, 53:39.

inessential needs seem essential, and in place of the four things of which he used to be in need, modern civilized man is now in need of twenty. And it is only two out of twenty who can satisfy those needs in a totally licit way; eighteen remain in need in some way.

That is to say, modern civilization greatly impoverishes man. Because of the needs, it drives man to wrongdoing and illicit gain. It perpetually encourages the wretched lower classes to challenge the upper classes. It has abandoned the Qur'an's sacred fundamental law making the payment of *zakat* obligatory and prohibiting usury and interest, which ensured that the lower classes were obedient towards the upper classes and the upper classes were sympathetic towards the lower classes, and encouraged the bourgeousie to tyranny and the poor to revolt. It destroyed the tranquillity of mankind.

Second Point: Since the wonders of modern civilization are each a dominical bounty, they require real thanks and to be utililized for the benefit of mankind. But now we see that since they have encouraged a significant number of people to be lazy and indulge in vice, and have given them the wish to heed their desires in ease and comfort; they have destroyed these people's eagerness for effort and endeavour. And by way of dissatisfaction and extravagance, they have driven them to dissipation, wastefulness, tyranny, and what is unlawful.

For example, as it says in A Key to the World of the Risale-i Nur, although the radio is a great bounty and demands thanks in the form of being used for the good of mankind, since four fifths of it are used on unnecessary, meaningless trivia, it has encouraged idleness and depravity, and destroyed the eagerness for work. I myself even have seen that of a number of most beneficial marvels, which should be used for endeavour and work and man's true benefits and needs, eight out of ten are urging man to indulge in pleasure and amusement, to satisfy his desires, and to be lazy, and only one of two of them being spent on essential needs. There are thousands of examples like these two small ones.

In Short: Since modern Western civilization has not truly heeded the revealed religions, it has both impoverished man and increased his needs. It has destroyed the principle of frugality and contentment, and increased wastefulness, greed, and covetousness. It has opened up the way to tyranny and what is unlawful. Through encouraging people to take advantage of the means of dissipation, it has also cast those needy unfortunates into total laziness. It has destroyed the desire for effort and work. It has encouraged depravity and dissipation, and wasted their lives on useless things. Furthermore, it has made those needy and lazy people ill. Through abuse and prodigality, it has been the means of spreading a hundred sorts of diseases.

Mankind is constantly threatened by three awesome matters: severe needs, the desire for vice and dissipation, and death —and numerous illnesses, which perpetually remind him of death— which the atheistic currents that have awakened mankind through their infiltrating civilization show to be eternal extinction. All these cause mankind a Hell-like torment.

In the face of this ghastly calamity of mankind's, it is understood from signs and allusions of the Qur'an of Miraculous Exposition that with the awakening of its four hundred million students and its sacred, revealed fundamental laws, it will heal those three awesome wounds — as it did one thousand three hundred years ago; and if doomsday does not soon break loose, with its showing that rather than being external extinction, death resembles the despatch papers for the world of light, it will gain for mankind the happiness both of worldly life and of the life of the hereafter; and in the civilization that will grow out of the All-Wise Qur'an, the virtues of civilization will prevail over its evils; and unlike has happened up to the present, a part of religion will not be given as the bribe for part of civilization, but civilization will serve and assist those heavenly laws. As the All-Wise Qur'an indicates this, so awakened mankind awaits it from Divine mercy, and seeks it, and beseeches Divine mercy for it.

The Eternal One, He is the Eternal One!

S a i d N u r s i

* * *

Books from the Risale-i Nur, and about it and its author, published in English:

❏ THE SUPREME SIGN* (Revised edn.)
❏ RESURRECTION AND THE HEREAFTER*
❏ NATURE: CAUSE OR EFFECT?* (Revised edn.)
❏ BELIEF AND MAN* (Revised edn.)
❏ FRUITS FROM THE TREE OF LIGHT* (Revised edn.)
❏ THE MIRACLES OF MUHAMMAD* (Revised edn.)
❏ THE KEY TO BELIEF*
❏ MAN AND THE UNIVERSE* (Revised edn.)
❏ SINCERITY AND BROTHERHOOD*
❏ THE TONGUES OF REALITY*
❏ THE IMMORTALITY OF MAN'S SPIRIT*
❏ A GUIDE FOR YOUTH*
❏ THIRTY-THREE WINDOWS*
❏ THE SHORT WORDS*
❏ MESSAGE FOR THE SICK*
❏ ON RAMADAN, THANKS, AND FRUGALITY*
❏ THE DAMASCUS SERMON✣ (Revised and enlarged edn.)
❏ THE HIGHWAY OF THE PRACTICES OF THE PROPHET✣
❏ THE MIRACLES OF MUHAMMAD (With notes and sources)✣
❏ DIVINE DETERMINING (FATE AND DESTINY) AND MAN'S WILL IN ISLAM✣
❏ ISLAM, THE WEST, AND THE RISALE-I NUR*
❏ THE WORDS (1st Volume of Risale-i Nur—Hard Cover, Indexes)
❏ BEDIUZZAMAN SAID NURSI—LETTERS 1928-1932 (2nd Vol. of Risale-i Nur—Hard Cover, Indexes)
❏ THE FLASHES COLLECTION (3rd. Vol. of R. Nur—Hard Cover, Indexes)
❏ THE AUTHOR OF THE RISALE-I NUR, BEDIUZZAMAN SAID NURSI (Hard Cover, Illustrated, Indexes)
❏ SYMPOSIUM, BEDIUZZAMAN SAID NURSI
❏ PANEL, BEDIUZZAMAN SAID NURSI✣

* Pocket size (16.5x10.5cm.)
✣ Paperback (19.5x13.5cm.)

Distribution by:

- Sözler Publications, Nuruosmaniye Cad. Sorkun Han No: 28/2, Cağaloğlu, Istanbul, TURKEY   Tel: (0212) 527 7607; Fax: (0212) 520 82 31.

- Nur Publications, P.O. Box 15214, Scottsdale, AZ 85267-5214, U.S.A. Tel: 1-800-825-9027; Fax: (602) 493-9798

- Asya Verlags GmbH, Kempener Str. 54, 50733 Köln, GERMANY. Tel: (0221) 73 38 04 - 62 12 55 Fax: (0221) 732 58 23